THE HAKKÂRI MASSACRES

AN ANTHOLOGY OF DOCUMENTS RELATED TO MASSACRES AND DEPORTATION OF ASSYRIANS IN NORTHERN MESOPOTAMIA

Tatavla Publishing
Mesopotamia Series 2

Tatavla Publishing
Mesopotamia Series 2

Address
GPO Box 1944
SYDNEY NSW 2000

The Hakkâri Massacres: An Anthology of Documents
related to Massacres and Deportation of Assyrians in Northern Mesopotamia
By Racho Donef

Second edition, Paperback – published 2014
Printed in the United States of America.
Copyright © Racho Donef 2014

ISBN: 978-0-9874239-1-7
Cover design & layout: Cemil Gündoğan

All rights reserved. No part of this book may be reproduced or transmitted in any form or by any means, electronic or mechanical, including photocopying, recording, or by any information storage and retrieval system without the written permission of the author, except where permitted by law.

First edition: Bet-Froso & Bet-Prasa, Nsibin,
Ṭboco qamoyo: tëšrin-ḥaroyo 2009
Editor: Jan Bet-Şawoce

Cover photo: Reverend Basliel Aprim, courtesy of Atour; originally published in Brigadier-General J. G. Browne, '1937: The Assyrians: A Debt of Honour', The Geographical Magazine, Volume IV, No. 6, November 1936 - April 1937 Edition.

THE HAKKÂRI MASSACRES

AN ANTHOLOGY OF DOCUMENTS RELATED TO MASSACRES AND DEPORTATION OF ASSYRIANS IN NORTHERN MESOPOTAMIA

ETHNIC CLEANSING BY TURKEY 1924-25

Racho Donef

Translation of Turkish, French and Swedish texts by Racho Donef

Editor: Jan Bet-Şawoce

Tatavla Publishing
Mesopotamia Series 2

TABLE OF CONTENTS

PART A 7

   Assyrian Epos / Atour...9

   Prolegomena..11

   Preface to the first edition 13

   Kmo xabre 15

   Introduction 19

   Historical Background 22

   Assyrian Resistance..26

   Turkish historiography related to the events 29

   Assyrian Resistance War Folksong...31

   Documentary evidence..34

   Population surveys 41

   False promises 44

   Assyrian Resistance War Folksong...47

PART B 51

   DOCUMENT 1 53

   The Nestorian Uprising and its Suppression (12-28 September 1924) 53

      REASONS FOR THE UPRISING 55

         The Mosul question 55

         Turco-Iranian political relations 59

         Turco-Iraqi political relations..61

         Turco-Russian relations...62

         Activities undertaken by the English on the account of Mosul...........63

      THE UPRISING 65

         The situation before the uprising 65

         The Hangediği Incident (uprising)..66

      SUPPRESSION OPERATION 68

         Ministerial Council's decision concerning the suppression of the uprising 71

         Operation preparations...72

         Benefiting from the tribes 84

Other objectives concerning internal security 87
Desertion incidents among the forces 87
The course of events in the operation 88
Initial situation (8 September 1924) 88
The situation on 9 September 1924 92
The situation on 10 September 1924 94
11 September 1924 Situation 94
The situation on 12 September 1924 95
The situation on 13 September 1924 96
The situation on 14 September 1924 99
The situation on 15 September 1924 100
The situation on 16 September 1924 100
The situation on 17 September 1924 101
The situation on 19 September 1924 103
The situation on 20 September 1924 104
The situation on 21 September 1924 104
The situation on 22 September 1924 107

Conclusion 122

APPENDIX 1 123

PRIME MINISTER İSMET PASHA'S REPORT TO PRESIDENT GHAZI MUSTAFA KEMAL PASHA SUMMARISING THE STATE OF AFFAIRS UNTIL THE BEGINNING OF THE OPERATION 123

APPENDIX 2 126

THE GENERAL STAFF COMMAND REPORT DEMONSTRATING THE EARNESTNESS AND THE IMPORTANCE OF THE SITUATION IN THE NESTORIAN OPERATION 126

PART C 129

DOCUMENT 2 131

DOCUMENT FROM THE SWEDISH ARCHIVES CONCERNING THE GENERAL STAFF OPERATION AGAINST ASSYRIANS IN HAKKÂRI IN 1924 131

DOCUMENT 3 137

DOCUMENT FROM THE SWEDISH ARCHIVES 137

REGARDING DEPORTATION AND MASSACRES OF 137
    ASSYRIANS IN 1925 137
COLLECTION OF DOCUMENTS 4 143
    DOCUMENTS FROM THE SWEDISH ARCHIVES 143
    REGARDING DEPORTATION AND MASSACRES OF 143
    ASSYRIANS IN 1925 143
DOCUMENT 5 146
    TELEGRAM BY JOHAN LAIDONER CONCERNING TURCO-IRAQI BORDER DISPUTATIONS AND DEPORTATION OF CHRISTIANS 146
COLLECTION OF DOCUMENTS 6 148
    ARTICLES FROM TIME MAGAZINE 148
COLLECTION OF DOCUMENTS 7 152
    The Gertrude Bell Archive: The Letters 152
COLLECTION OF DOCUMENTS 8 156
    British House of Commons and 156
    House of Lords Hansards 156
COLLECTION OF DOCUMENTS 9 167
ARTICLES FROM THE TIMES 167
DOCUMENT 10 197
    LEAGUE OF NATION REPORT 197

PART A

An Assyrian bishop with his entourage on a hike
through the dispersed Assyrian townships

Assyrian Epos / Atour

1915

Once you drew swords in the fields
You took over hundreds of cities and fortresses
You spit fire to the country of the enemy
You would defeat the world, Assyria

Once your name traversed in the tongues
Kings were in trouble with you
Nations bowed to your command
They would say the command is yours, Assyria

You were the blessed glory of Asia
You were the world's utmost example to imitate
You were the world's greatest nation
Where is that glory, that honor, Assyria?

You were the only one that would reach
Jewishdom and Egypt
In Persia and in the Ararat, in the hippodrome
Nineveh and Babil were Paris and London
Now you have no homeland, Assyria

For the Orient you were the crown of pride
You were famous with your arts
You were the merchant, the wealthy and the treasurer
Why impecunious now, poor Assyria?

You were the essence of wisdom, when you were absent
Let not the world become master of knowledge
A nation could not be mad about you
Yesteryear was dark, knower of the world

Why have you withdrawn now, Assyria?
Looking from above, Assyria cried
You were not supposed to be like this, Assyria
Think about our fallen state and be ashamed, Assyria

Remember, ancestral wishes were blessed
In the fields of war, impudence was necessary
It was the biggest problem on the heads of the enemies
They called you strong, Assyria

Indeed, your enemy is ignorance
Your blood meshed with the sleep of the heedlessness
Where is your exertion, don't you have life?
Go ahead, from now on, standing, Assyria

Remember to consider the homeland's sake
Let its affection rekindle your immortal heart
Consider this miserable state of the nation
Enough of sleeping, wake up, Assyria

Here ends the epos, son of Assyria
The brothers who read should contemplate your state
Oh, partner to my worry, oh, you are not
It is morning; wake up from now on, Sleeping Assyria
Standing Assyria would crush you otherwise

Source: Ṣawto d oṭuroye, Vol. 2, No. 12, Sanḥarib Bali, N.J. 1915.
Transcription from Garshuni: Ḥabib Be-Čeni
Editing: Jan Beṯ-Ṣawoce

Prolegomena

I decided to reorganise and reprint this anthology, primarily because the first edition of 2009 had a very limited print run. Also, the discovery of new documents and information necessitated a new edition.

The events that transpired in Hakkâri were tantamount to a crime against humanity and the Turkish Republic was responsible for this crime. The officers and soldiers who took part in the deportation and committed despicable acts, such as massacres, rape and looting, all belonged to the 62nd Regiment of the Turkish infantry. It was therefore an act committed by the regular army, which was sent by the Ankara Government for this purpose.

The historiographers, as named in the book, who consciously tried to misinform the Turkish public in relation to the atrocities that the army committed, can be regarded as complicit after the fact.

Preface to the first edition

The history of the Assyrian peoples in the Republic of Turkey is very little known. Dr. Racho Donef does us a real service by assembling and translating documents dealing with the Turkish military campaign against the Nestorian Assyrians of the Hakkari Mountains in 1924. This predates the military campaign against the Kurdish Shaikh Sait revolt, which is somewhat much more researched. General histories of modern Turkey do not mention this early repression of an already very decimated Christian minority.

The first part of this book is a translation of a history of the campaign written and published by the Turkish Army General Staff division for military history. It was for internal use and thus is rarely found in any library. This work is based on thorough research in the Turkish military history archives, and thus has the bias that any such sources have. There is no sympathy for the enemy and the purpose of the campaign is ethnic cleansing of a region – Hakkari – that was traditionally dominated by the Nestorian Assyrian tribes. This region was under dispute as the border between Turkey and British mandate Iraq was still unsettled and the British had vaguely promised the Assyrians an autonomous homeland which the Assyrians hoped would include Hakkari. Thus the Turkish military campaign was mounted in order to check a small Assyrian force that had entered Hakkari in order to give greater legitimacy to the claim to include it in a future Assyrian state.

The Republic of Turkey, under president Kemal Atatürk, responded by a massive build-up of army units and they crushed the Assyrian forces and ethnically cleansed the region of whatever Assyrians had managed to remain in place after the 1915 genocide.

The second part of the book prints documents from the archives of the British and Swedish foreign services. These reports give additional information about how European states judged the ability of the Assyrians to build a state, and their opinion of the policy of the Turkish Republic towards one of its smallest minorities.

David Gaunt
Professor of History
Södertörn University, 2009

Kmo xabre

I dawle dat tërk, bu Sayfo dan 1915, qṭila w maqṭela ğalabe came. Qšëcla an armënoye, aş şëroye madënḥoye w macërboye, ar rum, ap ponṭus, ač čalkoye, ah hëḏoye, aq qarač,... Mën hawi, briṭo kula, ḥzela b cayna. I oşmanliye, sëmwola suj rabo, mqabël di nošuṭo. Ad duwal rabe,[1] bi šato dan 1915, frëswolle buyono lu cëlmo bu medano. Bu buyono, mërwolle, "*Bëṭër mu ḥarb gëd mijazyo Tërkiya!*" Du šrolo, sim ğalabe ḥëḏriyat, sim ğalabe ytawyoṭo; talye w galye.

Rağam du medano, at tërk mdawamme bi taḥrasto d këtwolën qumayye. Bu Sayfo qaflat qaflat maqṭëliwo. Bëṭër mu Sayfo, han naqqa ḥa b ḥa maqṭëliwo. Qṭëlle ar riše d faliti mu Sayfo, kulle, bëṭër mu Sayfo. I waḏife du qaṭlano, xëd meqëm, bëṭër ste, li *Taškilati-Maxşuşa* mdawmola.

Bu zabno du Sayfo, Anwar Paša w Ṭalcat Paša, hënnewën b riše di *Taškilati-Maxşuşa*. Bëṭër mëd mahzamme l Almanya, i rišuṭo mëdole l Kamal. La'an meqëm huwwe ste ḥa mah hadomaydawe, idoṭe mganbëlewën bu admo d ğalabe noše.

Kamal bi šato dan 1923, sëmle i dawle jëmhuriye. Maqëmle i xalifatiye, i šëlṭonuṭo, bu ëšmo i ṭayuṭo... Amma u meḥo di dabara du qaṭlo w ṭëqṭilo ṭrele, u mdawamle acle. Ar riše qaṭole di Taškilati-Maxşuşa kulle, maltëmile lë ḥdore. Sëmle kulle mdabrone rabe, bu mëjlës w larwal du mëjlës. Kul rišo, Kamal, huwwe b iḏe mcayanwole. "... b Tërkiya kula, dlo qanunat d dabara-ḥšërto, bas lašan u madënḥo, mšayëc waliye [w qaymaqamin] b şalaḥiyat ğalabe cloye lašan dë mšayṭëri"[2] d maqwën i mekanizma du ḏëlëm, du qaṭlo w du ṭëqṭilo.

"Bëṭër mu Sayfo, Aṭaturk, mcayanwole l kul walaye w l kul qaḏa "markaz qumandani".[3] U qumandanano, b kul mede aşël huwwewe. Kšonëq, knoḥër, kqoṭël, ḥokëm, kmarfe,... U qanun huwwewe! Harke, mën kluzamle, huwwe b iḏe samwole. Ğer latwo! U mëštaylono du caskar ste w du culmoyo ste huwwewe. Mëḥšawwo kul mede. U qumandanano, u wakilo d Kamal'we.

B Mëḏyaḏ këtwo ḥa hawxa, markaz qumandani. Fašwo bab bote Bë-Bësse. Kul nošo, "markaz qumandani" qurewole. B ëšme du šrolo, nošo lë majrewo d qurewole. An noše maḥët-wolën ëšme "Allahsız qumandan!"[4] U ḥa d cubarwo l gabe, dcoro latwole.

Cammi Ëllo, mšaqconowe, samwo qunedër. Sëmlewole boṭ di caskariye ğal-

---

1. Gust Wolfgang, *Der völkermord an den Armeniern*, dok. 1915-06-06-DE-001; PA-AA/R 14086; A 17493, BoKon/169; A 53a, 3467; ṭebo bu telğëraf, 1993.
2. Ayaz Şerif Eşref, *Geçmişten Bugüne Savur*, Savur Belediyesi Yayınları, 2003, f. 80.
3. Qumandan du markaz, yacni di dukṭo kula.
4. Yacni u "Qumandan këfuro!".

abe šafiro.

B ḥa may yawme, bi šawṯaydan, ëmmiwola "Bë-Malke Mire," bu bayto daj jiran diḏan, Bë-Maqsi Murad ṯiqo damančaye. Babi muxtarwe. Xayifo qralle l su markaz qumandani. Mšayalle mene bi ifade, "Ayko ṯiqo i damančaye? Qay w l man ṯëqole?" Madcarle aclayye omër "Lë kuḏacno!" Grëšše li falaqa, bay yawme mcaḏabbe.

Cammi Ëllo šamëc bi masale, xayifo azze l gab u markaz qumandani. U qumandan uḏacwo l cammi mu boṯ caskari d sëmlewole. Hedi marfele babi w dlo, gëd maqṯewole."[5]

Cayni mede b Hakkari, këtwo wali ëšme Xalil Rëfcat Beg [Halil Rıfat Bey]. Bi dukṯo, u mëštaylono d kul mede, huwwewe. Këtwole amro acme më Canqara, më Kamal, m'adëb ad dëkoṯanëk dlo raḥme! Wali Xalil hawxa samwo. Mšayacwo dayëm i caskar cal aq qëryawoṯo daš šëroye madënḥoye. I caskar, uṯyowa, mëskowa ar riše daq qëryawoṯo, cal iḏayye, kurxiwo cal u tëltimo du silaḥ. I qriṯo d uḏciwo silaḥ latla, guršiwo ar rabayḏa li falaqa. Bay yawme mëḥanwolën bi qriṯo. Ag gawre ḥrene, mi zëcṯo mahzëmiwo mi qriṯo. Bi qriṯo fašwo niše w nacime.

I caskar amṯiyowa ḥëjje, *kito gabayxu heš silaḥ*! Kurxowa bab bote. B gawe dab bote, bi zoriye mëskiwo an abnoṯo w an niše, cëmliwo acmayye l qul dan nacimaṯṯe. Bu karano, xulqiwo ruḥo di zëcṯo b gawe dan noše. Bëṯër aš šëroye tayhiwo, ëzzënwo l ğer dëkoṯo mu ḏëlëm.

Bi qriṯo dë Txuma, cabiro i caskar w hawxa rjëmla cal an niše. Ag gawre mahzamwolën lu ṯuro. Bëṯër bë kmo yawme, azze xabro lag gawre şëroye, i caskar mën sëmla ban niše di qriṯo?

I caskar, acma u wali, azzën l riše dag gawre lu ṯuro. Bu ṯuro hawi mḥoyo bayn li caskar w lag gawre şëroye. Aš şëroye barimi cal i caskar, xrëzze hën w jrëḥḥe hën. U wali jriḥo maxlašle ruḥe. Bëṯër mi ḥadisaṯe, Canqara mšayacla quwwat di caskar cal aq qëryawoṯo b Ṯurcabdin w bab Boṯa.

Heš meqëm mi ḥadisaṯe b ğalabe, bu mëjlës, Kamalo, 12 ṯëbbax 1923, kyotëw cam Jacfar Ṯayyar Paša. Jacfar Paša bu zabnano qoyumo d Adırna´yo [Edirne] bu mëjlës. Kamal harke, kmaḥke l Jacfar Paša yarixo i masale daš şëroye madënḥoye. Kumarle: *Hani klozëm b naqla ḥḏo d mët-loyi! W dlo, bu mëstaqbël dayëm gëd makiwi rišayna!* Jacfar Paša komër l Kamalo: *Ṯrayya acli w hat lë ḥarulox!* Kamalo kumarle: *Zaṯan ëno, mawxa mnaqëlilox! I masalaṯe, latyo hawxa masale hayalla, kul qumandan ste laybe d samla! Mawxa, këtli awla aclox!*[6] Bëṯër Jacfar Paša mcayën l Omid qumandan lu Qolordi daš 7.

Jacfar Paša aṯi l Omid, markawle ḥudro b ëšme d Musul´u Kurtarma Komisyonu[7] [Ḥudro Lašan u Tëxlişo d Mawşal]. Harke bu ḥudrano, xëd hadome, Jacfar Paša maltamle am muxalëf di dawle du Cëraq, m'aydone d Kamal, cësekër, siyasiye, riše d cašëryoṯo. Jacfar Paša, lašan i "waḏife tarixiyaṯe" bdele kmarkëw w këmcadël bu Qolordi, bëṯër sëmle calaqa cam u cëlmo[8] [maltamle čatawiye].

---

5. Qëbolo cam Jëjo Cabdiyo [1925-2001], b tamëz 2000.
6. Kodal Tahir, Paylaşılmayan Toprak, Yeditepe, 2005, İstanbul, f. 174.
7. Dr. Qassam Kh. Al-Jumaily & Doç. Dr. İzzet Toprak, Irak ve Kemalizm Hareketi (1919-1923), Atatürk Araştırma Merkezi, 1999, Ankara, f. 105.
8. Doç. Dr. Keleş Zülal, Cafer Tayyar Paşa, Atatürk Araştırma Merkezi Dergisi, sayı: 44, C. 15, Temmuz 1999.

Ač čatawiye d markawle Jacfar Paša, kulle mac cašëryoṯo dac carab w dak kurmanjwën. Hani bdalle blalyawoṯo, khujmi cal aq qëryawoṯo daş şëroye. Hawxa hjome kowe bay yawme w baš šabe. Ğalabe qëryawoṯo qadiri dë mdafci cal ruḥayye. Mdayanne qum dač čatawiye. I dawle ḥzela rišo lë kmënfëq acmayye, rasmi, cal u darbo du ṭboco-froso, frësla "An naşṯërnoye sëmme cësyan!" Han naqqa mšadro i caskar baq qaflat aclayye.

I ḥkume lašan d dayšo u cësyan, hiyya, më zawno ğalabe yarixo, huwwola i waḏife du medano l Jacfar Ṭayyar Paša. B zabno karyo dëšle u cësyan. Jacfar Paša, u cësyanano, bu zëyudo cal iḏe daq quwwat milliye [čatawiye] mdašdašle.[9]

Brito bdela kmacliyo ḥës diḏa cal Canqara w cal i ḥkume kamaliye. A mgale rabe b Awruppa b Camariqa bdalle kkëṯwi cal u qaṯlo d kowe mqabël daş şëroye b Beṯ-Nahrin i clayto. Mi Knëšto dan Ëmwoṯo [KM] mšayëc E. Af Wirsén u swedi, acme hayye lu Cëraq. Tamo karixi, mšayalle w maltamme maḏco, mën hawi. Bu kṯowayḏe Wirsén[10] komër hawxa: *Laqina cam kuhne bu darğo cloye bayn da mšiḥoye. Ba ḥkeyat d maḥkalle cal u ḏëlëm dat tërk w di ḥkumaṯṯe, manṭarre u përč d qarcayna.* Hawxa mašfalle aq qëryawoṯo daş şëroye bi mënṯëqa dab Boṭa.

I dawle d Kamal lë kalyo cal haṯe, mdawamla b kul dukṯo cal aş şëroye bu qaṯlo w bu ḥëwtoko. B Ṭurcabdin, b Beṯ-Zabday, b Urhoy, b Omid, b Mërde,.. Bi šato d bëṯër, manḥatla caskar w čatawiye cal aq qëryawoṯo du Garbyo b Beṯ-Nahrin i taḥtayto ste. Sëmla Sayfo haṯo. Hawxa ṭrela i arco d Beṯ-Nahrin xulyo mam morayḏa.

Harke bu kṯowano, bu zabnano mën hawi, kulle cam dokumane kmëfrosi w kmëgloyo i foṯo šrolo d këtla li dawle d Kamal mqabël du camayḏan.

Aḥuno Racho Donef, bu aşël rum mi Qësṭantiniye'yo, zabno yarixo kcowëd cal u šëwolo daş şëroye. Harke ste, hawile tacbo w jëhodo ğalabe rabo, hul d sim u kṯowano. Këmqadamnole, mac cëmqe d lebi, tawëdyoṯo.

Jan Beṯ-Şawoce
Madrašto Cëlayto d Södertörn
Tëšrin-ḥaroyo 2009

---

9. Cayni mgalṯo.
10. Wirsen af E., Från Balkan Till Berlin, Albert Bonniers Förlag, Stockholm, 1943, f. 123.

Introduction

This book consists of a collection of documents concerning the deportation and massacres of the "Nestorian" Assyrians (but also "Jacobites" and Chaldeans) in 1924-25, and the boundary dispute between Iraq and Turkey which affected the Assyrians in the extreme. Having being subjected to genocide during the war, they had to endure further massacres which depleted the number of Assyrians in the Hakkâri region and eradicated their presence.

There are two major incidents which concerns the Assyrians of Hakkâri in this period:

i) the September 1924 attacks on the Nestorians, registered as 'Nestorian uprising' in the official Turkish historiography; and,

ii) the deportations and massacres of Assyrians in September 1925.

It is the dual aim of this book to challenge the official Turkish historiography propaganda presenting the events of 1924-25 as simply a 'Nestorian uprising' that needed to be suppressed and document the reality of the brutal deportations and massacres which took place in 1925.

The first document in the appendix (Document 1) is a translation of a detailed report concerning the Nestorian Assyrian "uprising" in Hakkâri in 1924.[11] This report was published in 1972 by the Turkish Military History Chairmanship of General Staff (*Genelkurmay Harp Tarihi Başkanlığı*), and as such the report is entirely from the point of view of the General Staff Command. Nonetheless, as the extant research material about this period is relatively scant, the report still constitutes a valuable source for researchers interested in Assyrian matters. Consequently, it is extremely beneficial to examine this document.

Although the report was published in 1972, its provenance is likely to be closer to the period when the suppression operation took place in 1924. There are three reasons which may lead to such conclusion:

i) the many syntactical and even spelling errors suggests that the anonymous rapporteur ["the Rapporteur" hereafter], or the trans-

---

11. *Türkiye Cumhuriyetinde Ayaklanmalar*, T.C. Genelkurmay Harp Tarihi Başkanlığı Resmi Yayınları, Seri No: 8, Ankara, 1972, pp 19-77 and 483-86; document provided by Jan Beṯ-Şawoce.

literator, had difficulties in adjusting from Ottoman Turkish to the newly Latinised Turkish script;[12]

ii) the conclusion of the Rapporteur that "the Turkish forces could not achieve success to affect a decisive resolution ... on the insurgents ...". Since after the incident in 1924 there were not many Nestorians left in Turkey, at least not in sufficient numbers to cause problems, the report must have been produced in times of uncertainty, not in the 1970s. The remaining Nestorian Assyrians were deported in 1925. It is therefore probable the report was produced in 1924-25 before the September-December 1925 deportations and massacres; and,

iii) the document contains two reports by İsmet and Fevzi Pashas, related to the events, dated 1924.

The Rapporteur places the 1924 incidents in the context of the League of Nations' discussions about the future of Mosul, which is part of Iraq today. In the negotiations, the British proposed for Hakkâri to be part of Mosul, something that the Turkish side opposed. According to Fred Aprim, "[t]he British maintained their stand regarding Mosul and added the Hakkâri Vilayet [Province] to their claim, too, in order to protect the Assyrian Christians."[13]

Although we may not discount the possibility that the British may have wanted to repay their debt to the Assyrians for participating in the War on their side, the British record of looking after their own national interests, before and since the incident, suggests otherwise. British national interests took precedence over those of the Assyrians. The Simele massacres of Assyrians in 1933 by the Iraqi Arabs, which aimed to obliterate the Assyrians, illustrate this attitude.

The anonymous Rapporteur ignores the wider context of the massacres that took place during World War I, and the attempt by the Assyrians to salvage something out of the lost homeland, is depicted as an act of banditry and treachery. In the official historiography, the so-called Turkish Independence or Liberation War (*Kurtuluş Savaşı*), is consistently represented as a legitimate and heroic act, yet the liberation wars of other nations are regarded as treasonous. The ideology underpinning this notion is that the Turks are eternally worthy masters and the nations they once conquered should be their slaves forever. This thinking is the bedrock of Turkish nationalism.

The Rapporteur lacks a moral compass; focuses on desired outcomes irrespective of the human cost, which is characteristic of the early years

---

12. Officially adopted in 1928.
13. Fred Aprim, *Assyrians: from Bedr Khan to Saddam Hussein*, 2006, p. 139.

of the new regime. During this period, as well as ethnic cleansing (in Pontus and elsewhere), any kind of opposition to the regime was brutally suppressed often by using the method of summary execution through the mechanism of the Courts of Independence (*İstiklâl Mahkemeleri*).

In short, the Rapporteur is duplicitous, hypocritical as well as amoral. He posits the proposition that Kurds and Turks are brothers, yet his text juxtaposes strategies to use the Kurds, not share power with them. He condemns the English for using the Kurds, yet he suggests the same course of action to be followed by Turks. He alleges the English spread propaganda and confirms Turks did the same. He provides detailed numbers of wounded and killed on the Turkish side, even the number of animals in one case; yet only flippantly reports about the deaths of the Assyrians. All Turkish deaths count as martyrs, while Assyrian lives have no value in the eyes of the Rapporteur and the new Turkish Republic.

Historical Background

The First World War had devastated the Hakkâri Nestorians, who had managed to retain a relative independence within the boundaries of the Ottoman Empire for centuries.[14] After the war, Agha Petros, a commander of Assyrian troops during the First World War, in his detailed Memorandum for "an Assyrian Autonomous State in Iraq" in 1919, demanded a state in which the Assyrian language would be the official language.[15] Also, the genocide of 1915 was a subject (introduced by Armenian and Assyrian claims) both in the Paris Peace Conference and the Treaty of Sèvres negotiations in 1920.

The Assyrian academic, Dr Abraham Yohannan, who attended the Paris Peace Conference, on 29 March 1919, on behalf of American Assyrian Organisations, made a submission asking for an Assyrian State, originally to be under the mandate of the U.S.A or Great Britain.[16]

The National Assyrian Council of Transcaucasia, representing Assyrians living in the Caucasus, also called for an independent state, which combined parts of the Iranian and Ottoman Empires, where the majority of the Assyrians lived.[17]

In the San Remo Conference, Lord Curzon expressed Assyrian wishes.[18] Despite Assyrian efforts, the Treaty of Sèvres, which provided for an independent Kurdistan and Armenia, did not cater for the Assyrians. Only article 62, referring to the area of Kurdistan, stipulated that "[t]he scheme shall contain full safeguards for the protection of the Assyro-Chaldeans and other racial or religious minorities within these areas".[19] The Treaty of Sèvres is said to have been ratified by Sultan Mehmed VI, who only had symbolic power at that stage, but not by the provisional government of the nascent republic of Ankara.[20]

The Lausanne conference did not discuss Assyrian independence or autonomy to any meaningful extent. Turkey, Great Britain and France were negotiating about territory, influence and oil. For differing reasons, the Assyrian claims were of no importance to any of the parties.

As Joseph Yacoub notes, in Lausanne, the Turks objected to the participation of Assyrians. Lord Curzon who in the past had declared that

---

14. R. Donef, *Assyrians post-*Nineveh, Sydney, 2012, p. 86.
15. Memorandum by General Agha Petros in S.O. Dadesho, *The Assyrian National Question at the United Nations*, Modesto, California, 1987, pp. 82-87.
16. Serdar Sakin, H. Zeki Kapcı, 'İngiltere, Nasturiler ve İç Toprak Projesi (1919-1922)', *ATAM*, Vol. 5, No. 5, September 2013, p. 215.
17. *Ibid.*, pp. 215-16.
18. *Ibid.*, p. 216.
19. *The Treaty of Sèvres*, article 62, reproduced in Dadesho, *op.cit.*, p. 62.
20. There is an ongoing debate in Turkey as to whether the Sultan signed the Treaty, as hitherto has been argued by the Republicans.

"[t]he British Government will do whatever it can for the Assyrians who live under its area of influence", said to İsmet Pasha during the conference: "I hope that the Turkish Government will give full guarantee for the protection of language, schools, traditions and religion of the Assyrians". That was the extent of the British concerns, asking İsmet Pasha, known for his anti-Christian feelings, to protect Christian minorities.

It is perfectly clear that the British and the French were much more interested in oil than addressing Assyrian aspiration for statehood or even some form of autonomy. In the same conference, İsmet Pasha said of the Assyrians "Assyrians were treacherous and cruel to their Muslim neighbours".[21] Thus, the aggressor set the policy of denialism that was to be instituted as a fundamental governmental policy in years to come.

The Assyrian delegation in Lausanne made some effort to convince the Turkish delegation to let the Assyrian resettle in their homeland in Hakkâri. The Turkish delegation stubbornly rejected these approaches. Having rid itself of an ethnic element through systematic ethnic cleansing governed by the commensurate ideology, the new regime was not interested in repopulating parts of Anatolia with a Christian population, indigenous or not.

The Lausanne Telegraphs published by the Turkish Historical Society contains all the telegraphs exchanged between the Turkish delegation in Lausanne and the Turkish Government in Ankara.[22] The telegraphs reveal the resolve of the Turkish delegation not to entertain any thoughts of an Assyrian homeland in any form. The following two telegraphs best document this attitude.

Cable sent from İsmet İnönü, head of the Turkish delegation in Lausanne, to the Turkish Government.

No. 353 January 15, 1923
No. 230, 231

The head of the Assyrian-Chaldean delegation in Lausanne, Agha Petros visited me and made the following proposal:

1. To grant the sanjak of Hakkâri for the settlement of the Assyrian and Chaldean population. If this were not possible then to grant the entire Gavur [Gewar] or Çölemerik districts, as well as some parts of Başkale and Şemdinan.

2. He asked for the return [of the Assyrian Nestorians] who lived in Çölemerik and Gavur before the war and who migrated because of the situation; and in addition those Nestorians who are in Iran, Baghdad and other countries, in short all of the Assyrians and

---

21. Joseph Yacoub, *Asur Ulusal Sorunu*, Jönköping, 1993, p. 13.
22. B. Şimşir, *Lozan Telegrafları*, Vol. 1, Türk Tarih Kurumu, Ankara, 1990; *Lozan Telegrafları*, Vol. 2, Türk Tarih Kurumu, Ankara, 1994.

Nestorians, to return and live all together and under the facilitation of Turkey.

3. In the event that this condition was accepted, then the Assyrian-Nestorian delegation will declare that they have no claims against [issues with] Turkey. Furthermore, the Chaldeans who live in Mosul would ask for Mosul to be annexed to Turkey and that they would help us to achieve this end.

4. The head of the Assyrian-Chaldean delegation also added that once we reach agreement in Lausanne they are prepared for him or someone else to travel to Ankara.

5. Accordingly, we cannot make any commitments about the return of the helpless refugees and other Chaldeans living abroad. The Assyrian-Chaldeans can live in Turkey freely like other Turkish citizens. We can send the head of the delegation to Ankara to declare this. To this end, I wish that we send an Assyrian delegation from here to ensure that the Chaldean troops in Mosul work for our interests. It is said that during the General War Agha Petros, as a commander of the army of revenge, caused much damage to us. Does he still have authority? Is it possible for him to come? I request in writing that the order is carried out.

Cable sent by the Turkish Prime Minister Hüseyin Rauf to İsmet İnönü.

No. 368; Response to His Excellency İsmet Pasha
No. 278C; Response to 16/1/39 (see No. 3530) January 18, 1923

It is obvious that we would not approve the settlement of Assyrians and Chaldeans in our country. However, as long as we do not make any commitments and if it is beneficial to send Agha Petros away from Lausanne, he could be sent to Ankara and we inform you that said person was an interpreter in our Urmia Consulate and has Turkish citizenship.
Hüscyin Rauf

The perspective of the Turkish delegation in Lausanne, and the intention not to deliver justice to the Assyrians, can also be observed in the memoirs of Dr Rıza Nur, who was a member of the delegation. Rıza Nur wrote that the Assyrian question was put on the agenda without much notice, which to him suggested that the western powers wanted to catch the Turkish delegation unawares. One hour before the session, the agenda arrived stating "in today's session the Armenian, Assyrian, Chaldean delegates will be heard." Rıza Nur expresses his surprise and goes on to paint a picture of conspiracy against Turkey:

> Besides, I had only seen Armenians; now apparently there are Assyrians, Chaldeans who we do not know and do not think about. I was astonished; astounded. I got angry. They are playing games with us. . . . I will not participate in the session . . . . By that I am saying to these people . . . . Armenians, Assyrians are not states. We came to negotiate with states.[23]

Rıza Nur purported not to have been aware of Assyrians and therefore they had no right to be there. With this justification, the Assyrians were not allowed to negotiate. Rıza Nur articulated the same sentiments in the Grand National Assembly when the Lausanne Conference was discussed: "I could not recall them at all, the Chaldeans and the Assyrians and they wanted land as well", and added, "the Assyrians, Chaldeans are naturally finished".[24] The latter an obvious reference to the genocide perpetrated against the Assyrians during the War.

Incidentally, Rıza Nur also expresses his racist sentiments against Jews and declares that he does not like them as well as using derogatory terms not worthy of being reproduced.[25] This is to point out the calibre of the people who represented Turkey in Lausanne.

---

23. Dr Rıza Nur, *Lozan Barış Konferansının Perde Arkası (1922-1923)*, İstanbul, 2003, pp. 169-171.
24. T.B.M.M., *Gizli Celse Zabıtları*, Vol. IV, İstanbul, 1999, p. 7 [my emphasis].
25. *Ibid.*, p. 145.

Assyrian Resistance

In 1921, about 8,000 Assyrians moved back to Hakkâri but most of them were forced to Iraq. The British helped Assyrians to organise and perhaps have one more attempt for autonomy. Ostensibly, the incident, subject of the military report (Document 1), started with a group of Assyrians kidnapping the governor of Hakkâri in Hangediği on 7 August 1924. This was regarded as a *de facto* insurgency. However, even in the Turkish historiography, the fact that this was only a pretext for the Turkish Republic to act against the Nestorians, which was already decided, could not be concealed.[26] The Turkish Government intended to establish a border battalion between Gziro [Jazire] and Julamerk [Çölemerik] and the Nestorian Region "to prevent them [the Assyrians] from returning once they are deported."[27]

The newspapers *Hakimiyet-i Milliye* of 13 August 1924 and *İkdam* of 14 August 1924 reported the event as an act of banditry, and, in the case of Hakimiyet-i Milliye, in a small section of the second page.[28] The new state, which controlled the media, did not want to draw attention to regional conflicts, which presumably would have undermined the picture of cohesiveness it wanted to promote.

As there was no military presence in the Hakkâri Province before the incident, the government allocated massive forces for the task; the report meticulously provides details of these arrangements. It is difficult not to draw the conclusion that the response was clearly disproportionate to the threat. The Assyrian resistance was brutally suppressed within 16 days (12 – 28 September 1924).

In any case, the intention of the government was not just to suppress the rebellion but also to attack Mosul. The commander of the operation, Ja'fer (Caffer) Tayyar Pasha received instruction to that effect from the founder and the President of the new Republic, Mustafa Kemal.[29]

Caffer Tayyar Pasha was born in Kosovo. He pursued a career in the military and was involved in the suppression of national liberation movements of many ethnic groups living within the boundaries of the Ottoman Empire. In 1905, he attacked Bulgarian guerrillas and in 1908 was given the responsibility of suppressing an Albanian uprising. In 1909, Caffer Tayyar Pasha attacked Greeks in Aydın under the guise of Eşkiya Takip Kumandanlığı (Commandery of Bandit Pursuit).[30]

Caffer Tayyar Pasha (later Eğilmez) was also a parliamentary deputy in the 2nd period of the Grand National Assembly. Mustafa Kemal,

---

26. Yonca Anzerlioğlu, *Nastur îler*, Ankara, 2000, p. 135.
27. Tahir Kodal, *Paylaşılamıyan Toprak*, İstanbul, 2005, p. 248.
28. Anzerlioğlu, *op. cit.*, p. 136.
29. *Ibid.*, p. 151.
30. Zülal Keleş, 'Ca'fer Tayyar Paşa', *A.A.M.D.*, Ankara, 1999, Vol. XV, No. 44, July 1999, p. 543.

following a private conversation on 12 August 1923, appointed him as the Commander of the 7th Army Corps and allowed him to retain his seat in the Assembly.[31]

The kind of people who took part in this operation demonstrates that the government's intention was to function in the same way as the Teşkilatı Mahsusa - the Special Organization. Teşkilatı Mahsusa massacred Christians during the First World War using irregular gangs of thugs, which also operated against Arabs.[32] For example, Özdemir Bey, in all likelihood a Teşkilatı Mahsusa operative, had led his own detachment in operations against the English in Mosul between 1921 and 1923.[33]

Özdemir Bey's detachment of 1,000 members included one major, six captains, six first lieutenants, nine second lieutenants and six third lieutenants. More importantly, special attention was paid not to enlist Turkish officers to the detachment; instead, Arab tribes and Tunisian and Algerian soldiers were enlisted to form the detachment.[34] This attempt to distance the army somewhat from the detachment suggests it was entrusted with a contemptible task.

Özdemir Bey, a Circassian from Egypt, was not a soldier but an irregular and had committed acts, which even Ali Nadi Ünler, who glowingly reports his activities in 'Antab (later Gaziantep) during the "Turkish Liberation War", finds it hard not to mention. In a footnote, Ünler informs that Özdemir Bey had issued some orders during the war which were not compatible with the military service.[35] Ünler does not provide details as to the nature of these orders, but it would be safe to surmise that massacres would have been carried out against the local population in Mosul where he operated. Indeed, when Cevat (Çobanlı) Pasha, Commander of Jazira Front, met with Özdemir Bey, he sent a cipher to Headquarters on 30 April 1922, describing Özdemir Bey as good-hearted, pure and brave, but added that he was concerned about his entourage.[36]

Another person of dubious standing used by the Turkish Republic was İsmail Simko, leader of the Kurdish tribe Shikak. Simko had

---

31. Loc. cit.
32. For further information on Teşkilat-ı Mahsusa see R. Donef, "The Role of Teşkilat-ı Mahsusa (Special Organization) in the Genocide of 1915" in Tessa Hofmann, Matthias Bjørnlund and Vasileios Meichanetsidis (Eds) *Studies on the State Sponsored Campaign of Extermination of the Christians of Asia Minor (1912-1922) and Its Aftermath: History, Law, Memory*, New York & Athens, 2011, pp. 179-194.
33. Zekeriya Türkmen, 'Özdemir Bey'in Musul Harekâtı ve İngilizlerin Karşı Tedbirleri', *Atatürk Araştırma Merkezi Dergisi*, Vol. XVII, No. 49, March 2001, pp. 49-79.
34. *Ibid.*, p. 49.
35. Ali Nadi Ünler, *Türkün Kurtuluş Savaşında Gaziantep Savunması*, Ankara, 1969, p. 75f.
36. Türkmen, *op. cit.*, [my emphasis]

assassinated the Assyrian (Nestorian) Patriarch, Mar Šamcun in 1918.[37] İbrahim Avas, former deputy for Van, depicts Simko as a womaniser and immoral person and reports that he was suffering from gonorrhoea. According to Avas, Simko believed that his health condition would improve if he slept with virgin girls, which he captured when engaged in banditry. Avas reports that Simko came to Shemsdinan with 1,000 cavalry and in his nine-day stay violated 18 girls.[38]

Kâzım Karabekir, a commander in the Turkish Army, in his memoirs admits that he transferred Simko from the English and helped the Turkish forces against the Armenians and Nestorians in Anatolia.[39] In 1922, Simko was defeated by the Persian Brigadier-General Rezā Khan (later Shāh of Iran). When Simko and other chieftains escaped to Turkey, Simko's entourage consisted of 800 cavalrymen, two artilleries and 8,000 armed migrants in Başkale.[40]

It would be remiss not to include Fattah Bey in this list. Fattah Bey who, during the operation against the Assyrians in 1924, was in charge of a force gathered from a squadron of the 1st Cavalry Division Shirnakh and Gürün Kurdish tribes, was an Iraqi national who engaged in transactions against the government of Iraq.[41] While the Assyrians were regarded as traitors by the Turkish Government, the treachery of Fattah Bey against the newly founded Iraq was rewarded.

Finally, Kurdish tribal leader in Mosul, Uceymi Sadun Pasha[42], should also be mentioned. Uceymi Sadun Pasha was given the title of *Şeyhül Meşayih*[43] of Iraq by the Kemalists in 1919. By giving Uceymi Pasha a semi-official title such as this, Kemal hoped to use him in his endeavours. According to a secret memorandum from the Special Services Organisation Baghdad to Air H.Q.S British Forces in Iraq in 1922, Uceymi Pasha had urged Mustafa Kemal to attack Mosul, but the latter thought his forces were not sufficient for this venture.[44]

Later, Mustafa Kemal changed his policy on Mosul and tried to use Uceymi Pasha as part of the organisation for the suppression of the Nestorian Assyrians in Hakkâri. Eventually Uceymi Pasha and his entourage were settled in Urhoy [Urfa] where they were granted 12 villages belonging to Assyrians.[45] This arrangement was later formalised

---

37. See S.d.B. Mar Šamcun, *Doğu Asur Gelenekleri: Patrik Mar Šamcun'un Katli*, Södertälje, 1993.
38. İbrahim Avas, *Tarihi Hakikatler*, n. p., İstanbul, 2005, p. 70.
39. Kâzım Karabekir, *İstiklal Harbimiz*, Vol. I, İstanbul, 1995, p. 239.
40. Gökhan Çetinkaya, 'Milli Mücadele'den Cumhuriyet'e Türk-İran İlişkileri 1919- 1925', *ATAM*, 48, p. 800.
41. League of Nations, *Question of the Frontier Between Turkey and Iraq*, Geneva, C.400. M.147. 1925, p. 7.
42. Also known as Acemi Pasha.
43. Scholar of the scholars; most wise.
44. Qassam Kh. Al-Jumaily, *Irak ve Kemalizm Hareketi (1919-1923)*, Atatürk Araştırma Merkezi, Ankara, 1919, p. 79.
45. Orhan Koloğlu, *Mustafa Kemal'in Yanında İki Libyalı Lider*, Ankara, 1981, pp. 77-79.

via a decree: on 6 May 1926, the Ministerial Council decided Uceymi Pasha would be settled in the village of Germush [Garmuše] of 1688 square metres within the province of Urhoy.[46]

It has to be mentioned in passing, that part of the force which came to attack the Assyrians, including officers, were of Kurdish background. Of those officers, İhsan Nurî with four other Kurdish officers Rasim, Tewfik, Qorsit (Hursit) and Ali Rıza Bey, abandoned their posts and escaped to Iraq.[47] These officers, members of the illegal Kurdish organisation, Āzādī, absconded for the purposes of a Kurdish uprising. Cemil Gündoğan labels this incident as a mutiny on the account of involving military officers.[48]

In relation to the Hakkâri operation against the Nestorians Assyrians by the Turkish Army, Gündoğan cites three reasons: ethnic cleansing, enlisting the Kurds on the side of the Turkish Republic and stationing soldiers in Kurdistan.[49]

The suppression operation, which used substantial resources, had effectively ended the presence of the Nestorians who survived in the Hakkâri Mountains for centuries. Some Nestorians, who survived and stayed in the Goyani region, were subjected to deportation and massacres in 1925.

Turkish historiography related to the events

The September 1924 incidents were reported as a "Nestorian uprising", as reflected in a number of Turkish studies, which are reliant on the appended report of the General Staff (see Part B). Vedat Şadillili, erroneously setting the incidents entirely in the context of Kurdish movements, summarises the report without providing the source.[50] Another researcher, Suat Akgül, copies the entire report without naming it and adds very little to the study of the period.[51] Yonca Anzerlioğlu relies on Colonel Reşat Halli's book which, in turn, is largely based on the same report.[52] So does Tahir Kodal.[53]

More recently, Mehmet Perinçek revived interest in the incidents,

---

46. Ömer Osman Umar, *Türkiye-Suriye İlişkileri (1918-1940)*, Fırat Üniversitesi, Ortadoğu Araştırmaları Merkezi Yayınları, No. 3, Elazığ, 2003, s. 196.
47. Cemil Gündoğan, *1924 Beytüşşebap İsyanı ve Şeyh Sait Ayaklanmasına Etkileri*, İstanbul, 1994, p. 21. For detailed analysis of the action of the Kurdish officers see *passim*.
48. *Ibid.*, p. 15.
49. *Ibid.*, pp. 117-18.
50. Vedat Şadillili, *Kürtçülük Hareketleri ve İsyanlar*, Ankara, 1980.
51. Suat Akgül, *Musul Sorunu ve Nasturî İsyani*, Berikan, Ankara, 2001.
52. Reşat Halli, *Türkiye Cumhuriyetinde Ayaklanmalar (1923-38)*, Ankara, 1972.
53. Kodal, *op. cit., passim*.

predictably blaming the victims for the aggression.⁵⁴ His argument is that the uprising was facilitated by English (i.e. foreign) weapons, used by the Nestorians. Usually, the use of the word "foreign" in the discussions of Turkish history by official historiographers represents an indolent method, because it always implies a sinister plan against an innocent, gallant and courageous Turkish side. The use of English weapons by the Assyrians is not sufficient in itself to mount an argument that they were somewhat complicit in the massacres perpetrated against them. The "Liberation War" of Turkey, a concoction of official historiographers, is a source of pride and reference for those historiographers. Yet, the fact that the Turkish forces used French, Russian and English arms is omitted in the official narrative. If Perinçek wanted to use a more balanced approach to the "Nestorian uprising", it would not be sufficient to point to the provenance of the arms, as both sides, essentially, used foreign arms.

Perinçek also cites an Assyrian folk song in Kurdish, which registered the Assyrian resistance as "Süryanilerin isyani" (Assyrian uprising). Perinçek refers to the song's lyrics that the Tiyyari tribe had not paid taxes for seven years and that the English provided arms to the *Süryani*. From this folk song Perinçek tries to draw a conclusion of treachery and foreign intervention. Understandably, given space restriction, Perinçek reproduces only part of the folk song in his column. The entire folk song, translated from Kurdish to Turkish, for this publication is as follows:⁵⁵

---

54. Mehmet Perinçek, 'Bu da özgürlük sloganınız mı?' *Aydınlık*, 26 October 2012.
55. Translation from Kurdish Mehmet Emin Altoğ, edited by Jan Beṯ-Şawoce who also located the original publication and arranged the translation from Kurdish to Turkish. For the full text of the Kurdish folksong see O. C. Calilov, *İstoriçeskie Pesni Kurdov, Rossiyskaya Akademiya Nauk İnstitut Vostokovedeniya Sankt-Peterburgskiy Filial*, Sankt Peterburg, 2003, p. 133, vd., 144 vd., 157 vd., 458 vd., 471 vd., 478 vd., 491 vd.; This collection is an oral history work, based on different regional songs sung by local bards about resistance. These songs in Kurdish were sung by the Kurds, Armenians and Assyrians. Many of these bards were forced out to the Caucasus, Armenia, Georgia and then Russia, as a result of oppression in Turkey.

Assyrian Resistance War Folksong

1
179 (87) [Hakkâri 1924]

O, outgoing, outgoing O, O thou that goes

They say,
Kemal Pasha assembled his grand parliament in Ankara,
He commanded all great commanders and officers to gather and come to parliament.

Hey, wow-wow, wow-wow, wow-wow,
hey-hey Kemal Pasha

All commanders and officers gathered in the parliament,
Kemal Pasha said:
"it has been seven years since the Tiyyari Tribe rose against the state,
they never pay any tax to the state."

Hey, wow-wow, wow-wow, wow-wow,
hey-hey Kemal Pasha

Whoever assembles his army and his officers
and sets off immediately for the Tiyyari Straits,
I will make him a Pasha

Hey, wow-wow, wow-wow, wow-wow,
hey-hey Kemal Pasha

They say, Osman Pasha took his fifteen hundred soldiers
from Diyarbekir, in order to attack,
they set off, their direction towards the Valley of Goyi,
near Tiyyari

Hey, wow-wow, wow-wow, wow-wow,
hey-hey Kemal Pasha

In one of God's nights,
Osman Pasha established his tent and his soldiers
in the Goyi Valley
He is fixing his artillery and munitions there
in the direction across the Tiyyari.

Hey, wow-wow, wow-wow, wow-wow,
hey-hey Kemal Pasha

He is flying the flag of war
at the tip of his tent
Assyrians are awoken in the morning
What have they seen! A great military force
entered the valley

Hey, wow-wow, wow-wow, wow-wow,
hey-hey Kemal Pasha

Armed with shells,
They say, they have taken up English rifles
In the middle of the night they came out of their homes and reached
the Tiyyari Straits,
where the army was deployed

Hey, wow-wow, wow-wow, wow-wow,
hey-hey Kemal Pasha

So much of the sounds of the cannon and machine guns
I hear
By dawn, the large military force changed its
direction towards the Peš-Xabur River,
dispersed, fleeing

Hey, wow-wow, wow-wow, wow-wow,
hey-hey Kemal Pasha

Look at the desert especially
So many bodies of soldiers remain unclaimed
The cannons and ammunition still on the field
Osman Pasha's command division
set direction to Jazire

Hey, wow-wow, wow-wow, wow-wow,
hey-hey Kemal Pasha

They say, he went on the wire
He sent a telegram to Ankara, he says:
Kemal Pasha!
The Valley of Tiyyari proved too difficult for me!
Whatever I did, I could not manage it.
A greater force should be sent to me!

Hey, wow-wow, wow-wow, wow-wow,
hey-hey Kemal Pasha

They say that
Mustafa Kemal Pasha and İsmet Pasha got on the plane
Came through the Goyi Valley
and inspected Tiyyari with binoculars
So many bodies of soldiers, cannons and ammunition
remained at the dessert

Hey, wow-wow, wow-wow, wow-wow,
hey-hey Kemal Pasha

They say, Kemal Pasha came to Botan's Jazire,
Writing on a paper in the barracks,
which he threw out of the plane, and said:
Every officer and commander has become a traitor!
I will leave a bloody table
at the front of the gates of Diarbekr

Hey, wow-wow, wow-wow, wow-wow,
hey-hey Kemal Pasha

The heads of those officers and commanders I will put on the chopping block of independence.[56]

Hey, wow-wow, wow-wow, wow-wow,
hey-hey Kemal Pasha

---

56. A reference to the brutal Independence Tribunals.

Documentary evidence

Despite other Turkish sources cited above, the appended lengthy report (Document 1) is the most detailed source in Turkish for the events that led to the demise of Nestorians in Hakkâri in 1924. The newspaper articles of the period concerning the events simply echo the views of the military and political establishment of the day - given the control of the media by the new despotic state. A more realistic interpretation of the events is offered by the Swedish diplomat Johannes Kolmodin, who reported to the Swedish Foreign Minister on 11 October 1924. Kolmodin, also inserted a translation (from Turkish to French) from the *Hakimiyet-i Milliye* newspapers, which represented the official Turkish explanation of the events (see Document 2).

When Ankara proposed to send a governor for Hakkâri, the British protested and "nothing further has been heard of the matter; it was naturally presumed that the Turks accepted the British stand-point."[57] The Turkish Republic regarded Hakkâri as Turkish territory (and it must be said the Special Commission, set up by the League of Nations to investigate the border dispute, concurred with this view). Yet, the status of the Hakkâri was ambiguous, despite the pledging of the so-called National Pact (*Misak-i Milli*) of 1920, which fashioned even Mosul as Turkish Territory.

Fethi Bey in his declaration to the League of Nations put forward the following argument:[58]

> The allegation of Britain regarding the non-existence of administration Turkish in this part of the Province of Hakkâri is incorrect. This province has never been ceased to be administered by the Turkish authorities.
>
> The province of Hakkâri always belonged to Turkey and the Turkish State had no need to occupy it militarily.

This may be regarded as a valid point at first glance. However, the Turkish State had actually occupied Hakkâri militarily. This was precisely the scope of the operation carried out and documented the military operation report of the Chief of Staff (Document 1). The Turkish Republic occupied other territories, which it saw as part of its expanse. Indeed, Turkey occupied and annexed the Antioch province of Syria in 1939 and never gave up her claims over Mosul. It also occupied Cyprus and from time to time waged military incursions into the territories of Iraq and Iran, ostensibly in pursuit of Kurdish guerrillas.

Even the Rapporteur could not hide the fact that Nestorians were living in this area for centuries, in fact before the arrival of the Turks,

---

57. 'The Turkish Raids into Iraq', *The Times*, 30 September 1924.
58. *L'Europe Nouvelle*, 'Mossoul et la Société de Nations', September 1925, p. 58.

and acknowledges throughout the text: "part belonging to Nestorians", "suppress the Nestorians and throw them out of their land." "Nestorian borders".

The Times reported that:

> The Assyrian territory in question was at the time administered by neither British nor Turkish officials, but by the tribal councils of the Assyrians, who had returned thither in 1921 (Document 9b).

Furthermore, the Swedish diplomat Kolmodin noted that Turkey was not in effective possession of the Hakkâri province at the time, or at least not its southern and south-eastern parts. Kolmodin went on to state that Hakkâri was regarded as "no man's land" and that the British "had been accustomed to consider it as its sphere of influence".[59] The territory was regarded as Assyrian, ruled by a tribal council. Evidently, despite all the arguments concerning Hakkâri being part of the new Turkish Republic before the troops attacked the Assyrians, its status was still uncertain.

The attempt to install a governor brought about the result which the Turkish Government wanted. As *The Times* reported, the Turkish troops which occupied the territory crossed into Iraqi territory in pursuing Assyrians.[60] The military presence was a violation of Article 3 of the Lausanne Treaty which prohibited any military or other movement which would alter the status quo in the disputed territories.

The governor seemingly sought to cross Assyrian territory to "collect tribute" from a Kurdish leader, a brigand in Chal, and grant him the title of *Mudir*.[61] While the Turkish newspapers of the day and the General Staff report accused Nestorian Assyrians of banditry, the Republic's representative was under instruction to meet and bestow honours upon a proper brigand.

The 1925 massacres against the remaining Assyrians within the *status quo* borders are not mentioned in any of the Turkish studies identified above. In these studies, the incidents in 1924 are portrayed as a plot against Turkey by the Assyrians, who carried out an uprising the day before the Mosul question was to be discussed in the League of Nations. Yet, it was the Turkish troops which attacked the Assyrians in September 1925, before the border issue was to be discussed in the League of Nation. Turkish sources are silent on this shameful action. This is understandable: the attacks against a defenceless population by the forces of the state in 1925 could not be portrayed as suppression of rebels. As

---

59. Letter from Johannes Kolmodin, *Riksarkivet*, INK. UTRIKES DEPT, D. No 10 | 185, HP 33 B, 28 October 1924.
60. 'The Turkish Raids into Iraq', *The Times*, 30 September 1924.
61. 'Turks' invasion of Iraq', *The Times*, 13 October 1924; *Mudir* is a government appointee in charge of a *nahiye*, a division of *qaza/kaza*, itself a division of a province (*vilayet*).

Joseph notes, a Turkish force was sent into the district a few weeks before the arrival of the League of Nations Special Commission; it burned and plundered the reconstructed Christian villages, driving about 8,000 of their inhabitants southward into the Anglo-Iraqi territory.[62]

The ensuing massacres were brutal. As well as killing men and women, young and old, the troops sold Christian women and children to Kurdish villagers, raped Christian women and forced the Assyrians to march for days without food or even water. During their march, the Assyrians were forced to eat leaves and wild plants which affected their physical as well as mental health. This horrible march and deportation of the Assyrians and the details of the ordeal were comprehensively reported by an Assyrian priest of Chaldean faith, Father Paul Bedar. This document in French, retrieved from the Swedish Archives, is translated and appended as Document 3.[63]

Father Bedar's conclusion was that:

> [t]his is precisely the aim of the Turks, to eliminate the Christians by means of deportations, which make less noise than big massacres. They pretend to put a stop to imagined Christian intrigues; in fact the Turks by moving people from one place to another they intend to terminate, to exterminate them - and they succeed only too well! The old Ottoman did not know this refinement of cunning cruelty. Here, there is a cure seemingly sanctimonious, but terribly effective.

In other reports from the Swedish Archives, Swedish diplomats convey that 3,000 refugees arrived in Iraq by December 1925 and that the number was increasing every day (Document 4a).

Receiving reports about the atrocities, " … the Council of the League despatched General Laidoner, one time Commander-in-Chief of the Esthonian Army, at the head of a League commission to investigate British charges that the Turks have been deporting Christians over the Mosul frontier."[64]

Laidoner reported that "[t]he Turks committed atrocities [and] massacres on the Christian population" (Document 5). The Turkish response to Laidoner's report was predictable. The Foreign Affairs Minister Tevfik Rüştü, complained that General Laidoner did not limit his inquiry on incidents in the border as prescribed by the President of the Council. Rather than disputing the facts, the Minister was annoyed that Laidoner conducted the inquiry at all on the plight of the Assyrian refugees.

Tevfik Rüştü furthermore, claimed that the "Nestorians will always testify against Turkey" and thus brushed aside the testimonies of

---
62. John Joseph, *The Modern Assyrians of the Middle East*, Leiden, 2000, p. 176.
63. Document located by Jan Beṯ-Şawoce.
64. *Time*, Monday, 12 October 1925.

the refugees, and that "Turkey had alway complained about the threat which constituted armed Nestorians being close to the border." He then accused Nestorians of committing crimes, who when pursued by the Turkish troops having to cross the south of the Brussels line[65] "abandoned their possessions". The massacres, rapes, looting and the practice of slavery were disregarded and a "plausible" explanation was provided. It was not the fault of the perpetrators but of the victims themselves.[66]

The Prime Minister İsmet İnönü himself denied that any deportations took place, despite the *undeniable* evidence of the absence of Nestorians in Turkey post-operation, repeating the familiar lines about Nestorian brigands:

> A report of the debate in the Turkish National Assembly on December 12 on General Laidoner's Report is being circulated in London. According to this General Ismet Pasha, the Prime Minister, made a statement in which he asserted that as no Turkish assessors had accompanied the Laidoner Commission it was therefore incomplete and that he had merely been sent to invalidate the truths brought to light in the report of the previous Commission. Ismet Pasha described the "alleged deportation of Christians" as greatly exaggerated and said that atrocity-mongering was habitually practiced against the Turks by diplomatists. In any case the Christians in question were spies, brigands, and traitors, and the Nestorians, aided and abetted by the British government had kidnapped the families of Turkish officers. He added that some 500 trained men armed and fully equipped coming from the direction of Mosul had attacked the Turkish frontiers while the British Mediterranean Fleet had carried out a demonstration along the coast of Turkey. After questioning the accuracy of the maps used of the frontier as laid down by the representatives of the League of Nations at Geneva, and General Laidoner's reasons for deciding as to the position of certain villages, and for neglecting to consider certain Turkish complaints Ismet Pasha assured the Assembly that the findings of General Laidoner had no value.[67]

Having disputed the findings of the report then the Turkish side attacked the reporter's integrity: "[u]nofficially the Turks at Geneva inquired, 'How much did Laidoner get paid for his report?'"[68] In order to demonstrate the dispassionate nature of Laidoner, *The Times* wrote that "Turkish Atrocities of the perennially familiar type were reported by Laidoner, whose lack of sentimentality or easily shocked squeamishness is ably attested by the fact that he once ordered 130 Esthonian Communists shot in a batch because they were about to start a revolution."[69]

---

65. The Brussels Line was declared by the League of Nation's Council on October 29, 1924 as a provisional line delineating the frontier between Iraq and Turkey, assigning most of the territory to Iraq. The line followed almost exactly the northern border of the Mosul province; see *League of Nations Official Journal*, November 1924, p. 1659.
66. *Riksarkivet*, UD:s 1920 Års Dossie, HP Vol. 1480, 3-4, 1925, Mosul-frågan.
67. 'Ismet Pashas view on Laidoner report', *The Times*, 22 December 1925.
68. *The Times*, 28 December 1925,
69. *The Times*, 28 December 1925.

1) General Laidoner began by recalling that the Turks had refused his commission access to the region on the Turkish side of the Mosul frontier. He then went on to say that the commissioners had cross-examined refugees from this region before there was any possibility of their having been tampered with by British agents. In conclusion he expressed absolute certainty as to the material fact that the Turks have been deporting the non-Moslem inhabitants of this region with frightful barbarity.

Specific Charges: 1) In September the village of Merga was surrounded by 500 Turkish soldiers under Colonel Backy [Baki]. After separating the women from the men and children, the entire population was deported in two columns. Two men and three girls were shot without reason; five old women were buried alive under large stones because they were unable to keep up with the march.

2) At the village of Alto four men and seven women were killed, and all the comely women outraged during a forced march under Turkish guards to Be-Gawda.

3) During their deportation from Billo to Geznakh, a ten days' march, the women of Billo were separated each night from their husbands and families and violated by Turkish soldiers and officers, who did not hesitate to kill those who resisted.

4) The 62nd Regiment of Turkish infantry was responsible for these and innumerable other acts of violence and pillage. [Full texts of reports by the *Time Magazine* attached as Document 6a and Laidoner's full report as Document 10].

Gertrude Bell, a British Government functionary, archaeologist and adventurer, was privy to discussions about the Mosul question and the massacres against Assyrians. As well as receiving information personally from Laidoner, who confirmed the terrible massacres that were occurring, Gertrude Bell recounted that the Turkish troops crossed the status quo borders to kill Assyrians within the boundaries of Iraqi mandate territories, beyond the territories of the Turkish Republic (Collection of Documents 7).

The British Parliamentary Hansards indicate that during the discussions about the Mosul question, the cruelty against Assyrians by the Turkish troops was noted (Document 8c). Lord Parmour, on 21 December 1925, addressing the House of Lords, stated that "[t]he history of those deportations is very terrible to read. No one doubts the horrors to which General Laidoner refers. They are further emphasised by the report of his own staff, who personally investigated the condition

General Laidoner (right) and a Czechoslovak colleague Colonel Jač photographed in the mountains of Sinat during the investigation into the Turkish deportations of Christians in the Mosul area. Sinat is one of the places south of the Brussels Line from which the Christians had been driven ('The Turkish Deportation', *The Times*, 8 December 1925, p. 20).

of these deported Christians" (Document 8b).

The Times published a number of articles in 1924-25 covering both the raids by the Turkish troops in 1924 as well as the 1925 massacres. In 1925, their correspondent visited the area immediately south of the Brussels Line and reported the atrocious conditions in which the refugees found themselves. Despite the denial by the Turkish Prime Minister, *The Times* correspondent witnessed the devastation the deportations brought upon the Assyrians.[70] (See Document 9h).

Wirsén, Swedish Military Attaché in Constantinople in 1915, was one of the three members of the Investigation Commission, who were assigned to investigate the border issue.[71] As a member of the committee

---

70. 'Turks and Mosul Frontier', *The Times*, 30 October 1925; see Document 9h for the full text.
71. The other two members were Count Téléki, former Prime Minister of Hungary and Colonel Paulis from Belgium.

visited high ranking Assyrian clergy and was told of massacres by the Turkish. Wirsén noted that the Assyrians "having now suffered terrible fate . . . lived scattered in Mosul's northern region."[72] Wirsén knew of the massacres in 1915, through his meeting with Talât Pasha[73] and with Assyrian clergy in Mosul. Wirsén notes the committee "had no time . . . to visit the Assyrian refugees in Mosul who made a sad impression" and that the "only thing [they] could do was to recommend the Council's attention."

---

72. Einar af Wirsén, *Från Balkan Till Berlin*, Albert Bonniers Förlag, Stockolm, 1943, p. 123.
73. *Ibid.*, p. 112.

Population surveys

The General Staff report as well as other Turkish researchers suggests that the majority of the population in Mosul were Turkish and Kurdish. Notwithstanding the disingenuousness of counting Turks and Kurds as one nation when it suited the Turkish state, the British sources point out the Turkish population in Mosul constituted only 5% of the population. As expected, estimates of the ethnic make of the province vary.

The Turkish Government claimed 263,830 Kurds, 146,960 Turks, 43,210 Arabs, 18,000 Yezidis and 13,000 Christians and Jews.[74] In Turkish sources it is claimed that from the ethnographic point, the Turks and Kurds come from the same origin and they always constituted the majority. Here, the writer Anzerlioğlu asserts that the Turks, Turkic-Altaic people and the Kurds, Indo-Iranian peoples, are from the same origin,[75] which echoes the Turkish note to the Special Commission in 1925. It was also assumed, rather arrogantly, by the Turkish Government, that all the Kurds would have chosen to live in Iraq rather than in Turkey, while at the same time, the Sheikh Said uprising in 1925 was brutally put down by the Republican troops! Wirsén notes that although most Turks would have indeed prefer to live under the Turkish regime, a small number of Turks wished to stay in Iraq for economic reasons.[76]

The English claimed 424,720 Kurds, 65,895 Turks, 185,763 Arabs, 16,225 Jews, 30,000 Yezidis and 62,225 Christians lived in Mosul, while the Iraqi census provided the following figures: 494,007 Kurds, 166,941 Arabs, 38,652 Turks, 61,336 Christians, 11,897 Jews and 26,257 Yezidis.[77] Assyrian Yousif Malik in his book "the British betrayal of the Assyrians" claimed 99,300 Assyrians, 40,000 Yezidis, 9,000 Jews, 5,000 Armenians, 17,000 other non-Muslims, 20,000 Arabs and 190,000 Kurds.[78]

Although all the partisan estimates provide figures that support each side's cause, it is evident that the majority of the population was Kurdish and the number of Turks was relatively small. Also, it needs to be clarified that the population referred to as Turks were Turcomans, who are indeed of Turkic origin but not Turks. The Turkish Government stated that there were no differences of race, religion or customs between Turks and Kurds and that the two peoples, though they spoke different languages, formed one single unit.[79] In essence, the Turkish Government

---

74. League of Nations, *Question of the Frontier Between Turkey and Iraq, op. cit.*, p. 31.
75. Anzerlioğlu, *op. cit.*, p. 121.
76. Wirsén, *op. cit.*, p. 160.
77. League of Nations, *Question of the Frontier Between Turkey and Iraq*, op. cit., p. 31.
78. Quoted in Dadesho, *op. cit.*, n.p.
79. League of Nations, *Question of the Frontier Between Turkey and Iraq*, *op.cit*, p.43.

wanted Mosul included in the Republic even though it had negligible ethnic presence there.

The Commission provided more detailed estimates. The Province of Mosul was divided into three *livas* or *sanjaks*:

Table 1[80]

	Kirkuk	**Suleymaniye**	**Mosul**
Arabs	35,650	75	119,500
Kurds	47,500	189,900	88,000
Turks	26,100	-	9,750
Christians	2,400	-	55,000
Yezidi	-	-	26,200
Jews	-	1,550	7,550
Total	111,650	191,525	306,000

What stands out in this table is the small number of Turks living in Mosul at the time - less than 6% of the total population. This explains why the Turkish Government was keen to promote the idea of the brotherhood of Kurds and Turks, albeit until the desired outcome was achieved. This construct was to strengthen the argument for a combined majority of the two ethnic groups. The Turkish side also underrepresented the number of Christians (mostly Assyrians) which amounted to approximately 9.5% of the population.

Another table prepared by Wirsén in September 1925, in case the Little Zab forms the border, provides the following estimates (Document 8b):

Table 2[81]

	In Turkey		In Iraq
	In Mosul	Outside Mosul	
Kurds	-	210,000	285,900
Arabs	74,000	30,900	52,500
Turks	-	14,300	18,400

---

80. *Ibid.*, pp. 76-77.
81. *Riksarkivet*, UD:s 1920 Års Dossie HP Vol. 1481, 5-6, 1925, Mosul-frågan.

Christians	19,000	35,800	6,400
Yezidis	-	26,300	-
Jews	4,000	5,900	2,000

Wirsén notes that it is probable that no Kurds or Turks lived in the City of Mosul. Clearly, as Wirsén subsequent notes suggests, the number of Kurds, Arabs and Turks were exaggerated. Nevertheless, even in this estimation, the number of Turks was low on both sides of the border, lower than the Christians, the majority of which were Assyrians. Thus Turkey wanted to annex a part of Iraq where ethnic Turks at best were the sixth largest ethnic group. This point has been emphasised by Viscount Cecil of Chelwood, in the League of Nations sitting of 21 December 1925:

> I do not know whether it is realised how small a proportion of the population of the Vilayet of Mosul is Turkish. The proportion is about five per cent. The majority of the population are Kurdish, and next to them come Arabs - both, it is true, Mussulmans, but not especially acceptable to the strong Nationalist Turkish sentiment which prevails in Turkey at the present moment. Then come the Christians - there are, if I remember rightly, some 60,000 of them - then the Turks, who number, I think, some 40,000, and then smaller bodies of Yezidis, Jews and others (Document 8b).

False promises

The republican regime used other strategies to ensure that only Turks were entitled to a state. One tactic was to promise autonomy in order to receive the support of the ethnic groups, when required. Such autonomy, which did not come to fruition, was offered to Kurds. Similar promises were made to the Assyrians. In 1925, Assyrian leaders Malik Qambar and Agha Petros were in Geneva, they met with the Turkish Foreign Affairs Minister Rüştü Bey, who asked them to petition the League of Nations for Mosul to stay within Turkey and in return, the Assyrians would be granted autonomy:

> ... if you decide to withdraw your petition from the League of Nations, and help us to get back our control over Mosul, I will send you to the City of Ankara to meet personally with our great leader General Mustafa Kamal Pasha, the founder of the new Turkish republic who will promise you as an honourable man that he will give Mosul to you as an autonomous state where you will have self rule state with your language and culture.[82]

Even if the Assyrians petitioned the League of Nations Turkey would not have granted any sort of autonomy to the Assyrians. Autonomy was also promised to the Kurds by Mustafa Kemal himself for helping the Turks during the "Liberation War" but betrayed them once he no longer needed their support.[83]

Rüştü Bey told Malik Qambar and Agha Petros that "if you help England to get Mosul they will betray you again".[84] In the event, on this point, Rüştü Bey was right; once the British took possession over Mosul they indeed betrayed the Assyrians.

Finally, the tumultuous period for the Assyrians in Turkey ended with their deportation to Iraq. As well as enduring genocide during the First World War, the Assyrians were subjected to massacres in 1924-25, through operations which went beyond the boundaries of the Turkish Republic. In carrying out these operations the Republican troops showed themselves to be worthy successors of the Young Turks and the murderous regime of the Union and Progress Party (Ittihad) and its policy of extermination in the pursuit of a dream of a pure Turkish state, ethnically cleansed.

In 1928 Turkey declared an "amnesty" for people who were forced to leave their homeland in the South East of Turkey. However, the Turkish

---

82. Sam Parhad, *Beyond the Call of Duty*: the Biography of Malik Qambar of Jeelu, U.S.A., 1986, p. 44.
83. In 1990, a Turkish political magazine, *2000'e Doğru* (*Towards 2000*) managed to obtain secret state documents which contained the views of Mustafa Kemal on Kurdish autonomy. It is clear that Mustafa Kemal had, in fact, promised autonomy to the Kurds. It is also clear that this was a manoeuvre on his part to obtain their support in his struggle; see 'Atatürk: Kürtlere özerklik', [Atatürk: Autonomy to the Kurds], *2000'e Doğru*, 6 November 1988.
84. *Ibid.*, p. 46.

Ambassador in Iraq on 25 June 1928, declared that the amnesty did not include the Assyrians and if they were to try to return that they be punished.[85]

In conclusion, it can be said that both the British and the Turks used Assyrians in aid of their national interests. The League of Nations' special commission simply rubber stamped the *status quo* border possibly to avoid a new conflict between Turkey and Britain/Iraq.

The Assyrians missed yet another chance for autonomy or even independence. As a result, they were uprooted from their homelands and were subjected to further massacres in Iraq, in 1933.

The events in 1924-25 were a continuation of the calamity that befell upon the Assyrian nation, starting from the nineteenth century when in 1844, Bedir-Khan, the Kurdish leader, massacred Assyrians. In 1895, massacres against Christians, including Assyrians, took place *inter alia* in Omid [Diyarbakır],[86] and in 1909 in Adana. In 1915, widespread massacres and deportations - amounting to genocide - was committed in the Ottoman Empire. The Turkish Republic using similar methods uprooted the remaining Nestorians, but also Jacobite and Chaldean Assyrians in the Hakkâri Region.

According to French sources, in the month of February 1926 there was an insurrection in the region of Bitlis. This was denied in the *Hakimiyet-i Milliye* article of 17 February 1926, though the French sources insisted:

> Yet one month after we learned that the head of the Yezidis, Hatcho [Hajo], had risen against the government in the area of Midyat or Medeat (province of Mardin, northwest of the former vilayet of Mosul).
>
> Hatcho, which had already attitude of inquietude at the national struggle, was supported by Ali Saib Bey, the hero of Urfa and even showed evidence of loyalty during the insurrection of Chekh Said.
>
> According to the newspapers of 17 to 25 March 1926 the insurrection was confined to the triangle of Midyat-Jezire Ibn Omar-Nsibin. The resistance forces were composed of Yezidis and "Syrians" (specifically Syrian Catholics). By the end, much the insurrection was put down.[87]

As Swedish diplomat G.O. Wallenberg informed via a cable of 24 March 1926, the insurgency concluded when "Hatcho . . . appeared with his entourage in Dijarbekir to testify of allegiance to the Turkish Republic".[88]

---

85. Yakup Bilge, *Süryanilerin Kökeni ve Türkiyeli Süryaniler*, İstanbul, 1991, p. 114.
86. Father Ishak Armale, *Osmanernas och ung-turkarnas folkmord i norra Mesopotamien 1895 / 1914-18*, Södärtelje, 2005, pp. 52-74.
87. Ministère des Ètrangères, *Bulletin Périodique de la Press Turque*, No. 45, June 1926, p. 8.
88. *Riksarkivet*, UD:s Konstantinopel-beskickningen, 1920 års dossie, F3, Vol. 4, 1925-1929.

Perhaps the final chapter of the tragedy was to take place in Simele, in the newly constituted Iraqi Kingdom, this time in the hands of Arabs. The British complicity was a major factor in these events. Another Assyrian folk song laments this event:

Assyrian Resistance War Folksong

2
178 [Simele 1933]

Wow-wow, wow-wow, wow-wow

Mate, this is war, the war hit us
The British hapless, the French big traitor
There is no one coming to help and rescue
Over the of the Scapegrace Mountain[89]
Through the banks of the Peš-Xabur River
Around Derabun!

No one comes to the rescue!
The only hope, the only one to assist, is God above

Wow-wow, wow-wow, wow-wow

There was a battle in the heart of the Mountain
On the banks of Peš-Xabur River
Around Derabun, among the trees,
Malik Yaʻqo, with three cries,
He was calling Malik Lawko, Malik Ḥanna, Malik Išo:

Fathers, brothers . . .
You must submit yourselves to the Assyrian soldiers
Let's have this kind of manhood among us
Resist this day of days
Destroy the men [against us]
Lay their bodies down

Let's act so that
The French to pull out the injured and the bodies of the dead corpses by the truck load
from the centre of Scapegrace Mountain, around Derabun,
Whether they want it or not [It's up to them]
the bastards won't retrieve the injured

---

89. Be-xer in Kurdish.

Wow-wow, wow-wow, wow-wow

Mate, as a war is going on against us,
in the center of the Scapegrace Mountain
In two places around Derabun
Malik Ya'qo called upon the Assyrian soldiers with three cries:

Fathers, brothers . . .
You must submit yourselves to the Assyrian soldiers
Turn a hand once to your brothers, Assyrian soldiers
Take an aim to those who went to the mountain,
to the English

We are going to kill; avenge the heroes
The French are lurking in the heart of Scapegrace Mountain,
on the banks of Peš-Xabur River, around Derabun
Whether they retrieve the bodies of these injured
and the infirmed
They can no longer save the bodies of these dead [people]

What to do? This is a mayday call
We say "help", no help is forthcoming
Water ahead of us, the valley behind us
On our head the rattle of the automatic [machine guns]
the roar of aircraft
this nuisance wheezing of the planes
is a cry on the men
Because of thirst our mouths do not talk

The body is without strength from starvation
Our rescue is still far
In the heart of Scapegrace Mountain
On the banks of Peš-Xabur River
Around Derabun
Help is still far away, it is not coming to us
Our only hope is God above.

Wow - wow, wow - wow, wow - wow

Mate, at the heart of Scapegrace Mountain,
On these slopes
There is a great battle going on
Malik Ya'qo with three cries:

Malik Lawko, Malik Išo', Malik Ḥanna
Fathers, brothers ...
Make a call to the Assyrian soldiers
Let them take on their hands, their butts off the trees
Let them take aim on the British with the 5-throws

The day is today
On the banks of Peš-Xabur River
We'll act in such as way that
Let the French carry the bodies of the injured and infirmed by the truck load
Whether they take them or not
They can no longer save the bodies of these dead people

The tribes and districts of the Hakkâri Mountains

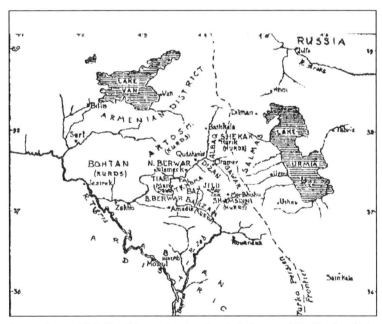

Source: Surma d Bait Mar Shimon, *Assyrian Church Customs and the Murder of Mar Shimun*, n.p, 1920; reproduced from D. Gaunt, J. Beth-Şawoce and R. Donef, *Massacres, Resistance, Protectors: Muslim Christian Relations in Eastern Anatolia during world war I*, Piscataway, New Jersey, Gorgias, Press, 2006.

PART B

A group of the Mountain Assyrian Maliks [chiefs], who served as advisers of the Nestorian (Assyrian Church of the East) Patriarch Mar Shimon Benyamin during the First World War; Rev. Joel E. Werda, The Flickering Light of Asia, 1920.

DOCUMENT 1
(Original text in Turkish)

The Nestorian Uprising and its Suppression[90]
(12-28 September 1924)

---

90. 'Nasturi Ayaklanması ve Sebepleri' in *Türkiye Cumhuriyetinde Ayaklanmalar*, T.C. Genelkurmay Harp Tarihi Başkanlığı Resmi Yayınları, Seri No: 8, Genelkurmay Basımevi, Ankara, 1972, pp. 19-77 and 483-86.

REASONS FOR THE UPRISING

The Mosul question

When no agreement was reached during the Lausanne Conference on whether the region of Mosul would join Turkey, in accordance to the Third Clause of the Lausanne Treaty, the matter of the designation of Turkish-Iraqi border was postponed.

Turkey's attitude against England on this matter, which needed to be resolved eventually, was thus:

Since peace was concluded, Turkey's attitude was dependent on England's policy on Turkey. It was true that the province of Mosul signified either strong ties between England and Turkey or a weapon they would use against each other. For Turkey, the Mosul question was primarily a national question. More than 66% of the population were Turks and Kurds. These two nations ruled the country jointly in Anatolia sharing completely a common fate. They could not leave their half a million indivisible brethren in Mosul to a foreign state, as tools of provocation and defeatism. If in the negotiations England were to insist on this matter, it would have been interpreted as mal intention against Turkey; in which case Turkey needed to treat the peace of Lausanne only as discussions and arrange her domestic and foreign policy accordingly.

It was for the reasons that the Mosul question was for Turkey an important and vital matter. Yet, for England, if she did not have mal intentions and determination against Turkey, Mosul was of secondary importance. Even if Mosul remained in Turkey, England would still have been satisfied, because, if Mosul were Turkish, England could have operated petroleum and other ore mines freely and securely. They should have known that Turkey's aim was to improve in the economic arena within her own national borders and did not nurture a thought of an attack on Iraq. Besides, if they wanted, a guarantee could have been given to them on this matter. Actually, if there was a thought of an attack by Turkey in Iraq, Mosul being controlled by England, would not have constituted a serious hurdle for Turkey.

As was seen in Lausanne, the most important evidence put forward by the English was the promise they made to Sharif Hussein[91] and the Arabs in the beginning of the war, on the grounds of the promise of mandate they received from the League of Nations. Yet, there was still no official document concerning the League of Nations' mandate granting Iraq to England. Even if it were granted, in accordance to Clause 22, Paragraph 4 of the League of Nations' agreement, it should have been granted after the peoples' vote concerning the mandatory state has been taken. In order for such a vote to be taken freely the country needed to be evacuated [of the English]. Until this was done, even if the League of Nations granted a mandate, it would not have been valid. Furthermore, it was necessary to prove that Mosul was part of Iraq. This aside, legally, it could not give to anybody else land belonging to Turkey. In this situation, the promise the English made to Sharif Hussein and the Arabs was of this nature and it was seen that Sharif Hussein's protestation on 1 October 1923 concerning the League of Nations decision on the mandate, constituted a proof that England could not use the promise made to him and the Arabs as evidence against Turkey.

-With an agreement on the Mosul issue:
the English would have operated the Mosul petroleum peacefully, in an area where security would have been provided by Turkey and transport petroleum safely through İskenderun Bay, which is the closest outlet from economic point of view;

-an English company could have operated one of the most important routes to India, the Anatolian railways; moreover it could have received concessions on Samsun-Sıvas-Omid and some lines in the East;

-[the English could have] procured other financial benefits from Turkey, other than these;

-by gaining the friendship of a state, which controls the Straits and has an influence on their brethren in the Caucasus, on Syria, and Islamic nations, England would have taken advantage of these opportunities.

Despite these specific advantages, it was understood from the Mosul question whether England wanted to be friends with Turkey. In the meantime, despite the pressure, threats and dispatching of soldiers, they could not control the Suleymaniye *sanjak*[92]. Local deputies were elect-

---

91. Hussein bin Ali, Sharif of Mecca was appointed by the Ottoman Empire to manage the holy places. Great Britain encouraged Sheriff Hussein to revolt against the empire and in return Great Britain promised to recognize the Arab independence.
92. Administrative subdivision of a Province (*Vilayet*) in the Ottoman Empire, governed by a *mutasarrif*.

ed from the sanjak and sent to the Grand National Assembly of Turkey. Nonetheless, because this related to the 3rd Clause of the Lausanne Treaty, Turkey did not admit them to the Assembly. Likewise, Mosul, even though it was under occupation, also sent deputies who were not admitted for the same reason.[93] All these events were demonstrating the reasons why England was avoiding a plebiscite. Despite everything, Turkey was determined to insist upon the plebiscite. If the issue was agreed upon in principle; the manner in which it would have been carried out and its details could have been negotiated and measures taken to satisfy both sides.

If the matter was accepted in principle, the details and measures could have been negotiated in a way that would have satisfied both sides. If the matter was going the way of being handled by the League of Nation, due to the influence of the English there, it was unknown to what extent could have been resolved in favour of Turkey. For this reason Turkey needed to pressure France and England earlier. In the negotiations, if the English rejected the option of the plebiscite, it would have been requested that the English propose an option based on the principles declared by the Allies during the war and later by Wilson. If they did not propose this principle and insisted on baseless foundations such as that they received promise of a mandate from the League of Nations and the promises they gave to the Arabs, it would have been declared openly that they were wrong [and] that they could not find a solution based on new principles. Subsequently, Turkey would have proposed that Mosul be divided according to the nations principle; i.e. the parts in which there was Turkish and Kurdish majority to be part of Turkey, the parts in which Arabs were in the majority to stay in Iraq.

The principles which would have harmonised the claims of both parties were not in contradiction of the Turkish and English delegations' statements. Undoubtedly, there were financial and transportation issues in the division to be made in this way. In the event that Turkey's and Iraq's territories could have become intermingled and interpenetration might have occurred, the two sides could have the right to military and commercial transportation through the territory of the other side. Accordingly, a number of special agreements could have been made on this matter.

Actually, there were already agreements in similar situations and

---

93. These deputies off ill-repute were Nuri Halil Agha (also known as Fat Nuri or Nuri the Brute), who was imprisoned several times; Suleiman Fehim Efendi who escaped to Turkey due to unresolved tax matters; and, Naib Zade Nuri Efendi who owed taxes to the Iraqi government and also escaped to Turkey. They later formed an association for the "Liberation of Mosul" under the leadership of Ja'fer Tayyar Pasha, the commander of the Nestorian suppression operation; Qassam Kh. Al-Jumaily, *Irak ve Kemalizm Hareketi (1919-1923)*, Atatürk Araştırma Merkezi, Ankara, 1919, p. 105.

recognising this type of right of way (East Prussia, Danzig[94], Turkey's use of the ports of İskenderun and Batum; the right of military transportation vested with Turkey in the Baghdad railway Meydani-Akbaz-Müslümiye-Chobanbey section and with France in the Nsibin section etc).

Turkey was seeing the Mosul question as a Turkish and Kurdish question and she was not planning to create difficulties for England on the matter of commercial concessions. The Turkish Petroleum matter could also have been resolved with this understanding. Yet, England's main objective on the Mosul question was:

-to control a Kurdish mass, which would have facilitated interference in the internal affairs in order to break up Turkey in the future to a great extent;

-at the same time, in this way, securely benefit from the petroleum mines;

-using Kurds against Arabs on the pretext of defending the Kurdish minority. In order to never leave Iraq, she kept creating more reasons.

No matter how constructive the policy Turkey observed was, certainly it would not harmonise with the policy English observed from the perspective of their interests only. For this reason, the bilateral negotiations conducted in Istanbul (Halich Conference)[95] did not bring about a resolution and the matter was referred to the League of Nations. Parallel to the negotiations, in order to create a *milieu* conducive to the achievement of their objectives, the English increased the underhanded activities they started. With the participation of the Americans too, through the missionaries and aid delegations, they made efforts to call upon the Armenians and Nestorians to return to the Province of Urmia, to make them a strong factor. Russia was striving to assist the Armenians to return to around the Turkish borders. As for Iran, she was put in a position of not acting outside the wish of these states, as she procured plenty of money from them.

There was no doubt that, again, through the plentiful assistance from these states, the Armenians and Assyrians, who concentrated in Urmia

---

94. The Free City of Danzig, present-day Gdańsk, Poland, was an autonomous Baltic port and city-state established on January 10, 1920, in accordance with the terms of Part III Section XI of the Treaty of Versailles of 1919, which split it off from Germany along with other German territories. It was placed under the League of Nations protection, with special economic rights reserved for Poland.
95. The Halich [Haliç] Conference [Golden Horne, Constantinople Conference] was conducted on 19 May 1924, in the building of the Ministry of the Navy in Halich, Istanbul, to resolve the Mosul Question and border issues between Iraq and Turkey. The Great Britain was represented by Sir Percy Cox and Turkey by the President of the Grand National Assembly, Fethi Okyar.

(in Rezaiye), under the protection of great states, such as England, America and Russia, were developing fast and would have become a dangerous force for Turkey.

This situation would have been detrimental in the future and dangerous for Iran, as much as for Turkey. Nonetheless, Iran did not have the intention or the ability to prevent this situation. They did not see a drawback in the settlement of the Armenians and Assyrians in Urmia and Salmas. The Christians who lived in the western border of Azerbaijan for many years and had connection to that land, had to leave their native country and move away to lands afar, because of the revolutions much earlier and the unexpected events of the First World War. As for now, seeing that safety was restored, they thought they were returning to their country. At that time, Iran which was completely under the influence of England, undoubtedly could not take this matter seriously. Yet Turkey was in the position to prevent this situation in the near future, on her own. For this, she first needed to take military measures in her borders and give a new direction to her diplomatic relations with Iran.

Turco-Iranian political relations

Iran's attitude towards Turkey presented itself as two opposed views: both for and against. Those who demonstrated negative attitude were statesmen who saw their national interest in English and American money. The policy these people observed was never a friendly one. Although this was the reality, the Iranian State administrators on the one hand felt the need to appear friendly to Turkey to develop financial and commercial ties; on the other hand they encouraged the tribes in the country to attack Turkey and fooling the tribes in Turkey to emigrate to Iranian territory. Likewise, on the pretext of an incident caused deliberately among the Kotur and Saray tribes, they continued to demonstrate an attitude, which was not suitable to friendship, and a hostile policy such as sending a team of cavalrymen to violate Turkish borders [just] as a show.

As the majority of the population was in reality composed of Turks, the Iranian state administrators so that this population one day did not turn its attention with national sentiments towards Turkey, since time immemorial took the path of traditional sectarian hostility. As this was not enough, lately they had absolutely forbid the teaching of Turkish in their schools. They also went as far as to teach history books which inculcated that the Turkish people in Iran were originally Persian who in the middle ages, during Turkish and Tatar raids, were forcibly Turkified.

It is because of this attitude that Turkey was almost never treated honestly by these people. At the same time, in order not to cause even bigger threat in the future, there was a benefit in looking to establish friendly relations with Iran, for there was no race unity in the Iranian State. In contrast, with the pressure coming from the north and the south and the effect of the events that occurred in Turkey, the national sentiments of many races were being strengthened, despite the efforts of the Iranian Government to the contrary. With this consideration, it was possible to think that this state would have disintegrated one day. If such situation eventuated, Turkey would have been encircled more extensively by more dangerous neighbours such as the Russians, the English and the Iranians and in a more extensive manner; such that the significance of the pain this would have caused was obvious. In order to prevent such situation from occurring - despite the continuing hostile attitudes - Turkey needed to think of solutions to refrain from any activity which would have facilitated the calamity of disintegration of Iran and consequently serving the English and Russian aspirations and reduce the hostile movements organised by the Iranian state administrators to the lowest level.

To achieve such a result, Turkey could have taken the following measures, which could have had an influence on Iran: the rendering of the Beyazıt-Erzurum-Trabzon transit road, which formed the Iran-Azerbaijan trade route, to a state where it could be useful, and until then to facilitate it by way of transferring custom processes from Kızıldize to Erzurum.

This situation was very important for Iran, because neither the Caucasus nor the Bagdad route was convenient for transportation of Azerbaijani goods, as safe and cheap as the Trabzon route. In this regard, by having this route open, the effect on the Iranian Government could have been quite great.

- The matter of the military service obligations of the Iranians in Turkey, and the Iranians that would come to settle in Turkey, to be settled in a way that favours the Iranians.

- Through the Turkish Foreign Affairs officers in Iran to explain periodically Turkish good intentions and state in detail the drawbacks which would come about if both governments worked against each other in a way that would serve English and Russian ambitions.

- Treating the Iranian Ambassador in Turkey differently.

- Resolution of the current matters in dispute, through a committee of bilateral representatives on the Iranian border, reviewed anew on the field.

If these and similar measures would have reduced to some extent, the Iranian Government's hostile attitude against the Turks, but despite Turkey's all good intentioned efforts Iran came to a point where she was disintegrating, then we would have obtained the opportunity as of then to please the Iranian Azerbaijani people, who would want to join Turkey. With this type of behaviour, even if it were up to a point, it would have been possible to gain the gratitude of the notables of the Iranian Government and especially the Prime Minister Reza Khan and consequently with their consent secretly take advantage of the most secure connection route between Van and Hakkâri provinces and Rewanduz and Suleymaniye regions, which pass through the Iranian border.

Despite all the efforts to be made to improve Turco-Iranian relations, if the Iranian Government's thoughts and attitudes did not change, and their hostile attitude against Turkey continued, then the Turks' attitude needed to change too. Such that, firstly, she would close the transit route, then send Simko - who is in Turkey as a political refugee - to Iran, through unofficial means. [He] would disperse the Armenians and Nestorians who concentrated around Urmia and Salmas, and also create new troubles for the Iranian Government, and this way it could have been possible to pressure Iran.

Contrary to the Iranian statesmen's negative attitude against Turkey, the people were entirely in favour of Turks: they wanted a Turco-Iranian alliance and were in the view that Iran could not survive on her own.

If Turkey followed an active policy of targeting the Iranian population, she would have succeeded to the extent of surpassing the English and Russian policies. That is, because Iranians were seeing Turkey as a liberator and a leader, with great interest were observing the events taking place in Turkey. Iranian *mujahedin* were pleased with the declaration of the Republic and the abolition of the Caliphate in Turkey, for they were in the belief that with the end of the Caliphate the Turco-Iranian relationship had extended even further. In the event that Turkey worked with a systematic program, within two to three years, even a Turco-Iranian military alliance could have been achieved and consequently would have obtained an important force and resource of wealth in the East.

Turco-Iraqi political relations

There were no demarcated *status quo* boundaries between Turkey and Iraq. As *status quo* boundaries Turkey was recognizing the line that was determined in accordance to the location of the Turkish forces in the

Armistice of Moudros[96] (20 km south of Suleymaniye – 15 km south of Bazwan – 5 km north of Altınköprü – 50 km south of Mosul – between Um uz-Zabe and ʹAyn ul-Tawahiyat – the line which goes through the environs of ʹAyn ul-Makhrube and reaches the Euphrates in 30 km of the southeast of Biret). Until the League of Nations made a definite decision on the Mosul question, the Iraqi forces were to retreat at least to the rear of the line that the English proposed after the Armistice (the Adrama Mountains in the Iranian border – 5 km south of Shehirpazar – 25 km south of Draniye – 40 km west of Zabıbekir and Rewanduz, which cuts through Fasruk and the immediate north of this river up to the point which forms a turn and follows this river in a line from there to Zakho). In contrast, it was accepted that the Turkish forces would not cross this line and the southern border of the Shemdinli district.[97]

Turco-Russian relations

Russia also had an eye on the regions the English wanted, to include them in her sphere of influence. [Russia] too had the ambition of taking them under her sovereignty through different means. For this reason, on the one hand [the Russians] were working to establish a Bolshevik organisation against the missionary organisation of the Americans; on the other hand, they were trying to use some influential Armenians on their behalf. Such that in these areas they were granting, the Armenians and Assyrians who owned large properties, credit from Russian banks to the extent that they would not be able to repay. This way they would have the opportunity to own these places and distribute them to their own men, and even bringing migrants from Yerevan and other places to reside and virtually create a colonial country dependent on her.

The aim of the Russian with these types of efforts was to have the upper hand on the English in Iran, at any cost, and just as in the Tsarist period, to hold Urmia and its environs.

In the end, if such a wide territory along the Turkish border became a Russian colony, it would have undoubtedly given birth to a new danger of bolshevism along the borders for the Turks.

---

96. The Armistice of Moudros (30 October 1918) ended the hostilities in the Middle Eastern theatre between the Ottoman Empire and the Allies of World War One. It was signed by the Minister of Marine Affairs Rauf Bey and the British Admiral Somerset Arthur Gough-Calthorpe, on board the HMS Agamemnon in Moudros (Μούδρος) harbor on the Greek island of Lemnos; Efraim Karsh and Inari Karsh, *Empires of the Sand*, Cambridge: MA, 2001, p. 327.
97. Shamizdin in Assyrian, Shemdinan in Kurdish.

Activities undertaken by the English on the account of Mosul

The English were pursuing a policy of establishing Kurdish, Armenian, Assyrian and Chaldean governments against Turkey and Russia before the resolution of the Mosul question.

To this end, as well as working for it through a variety of means, they also had Sıdda, who had great influence in Rewanduz, work on their behalf in exchange of a lot of money and other interests.[98] This way Sıdda who was serving English aspirations to reconcile Armenian and Assyrians with the Kurdish tribes along the border and trying to create a Kurdo-Armenian alliance and on this endeavour he was being assisted by some Kurds. That is because the Herki Kurdish tribe in winter housed their flocks and animals around Mosul, and other Kurds while the flocks were in Mosul were afraid that Sıdda would confiscate them; consequently they would be seen as subservient to Sıdda.

The English, in order to realise their insidious and secret plans followed the path of taking advantage of Armenians and Assyrians in Iraq. They armed their men and gathered their women and children from around Kerkuk [Beth-Slukh], Koysanjak, Arbil and Rewanduz to bring them to Urmia. Their aim was to form an important force against the Turks in Mosul and at the same time, through Sıdda, to establish a Kurdo-Armenian alliance under their mandate and create independent Kurdish and Armenian governments in name, though in practice, an English colony.

The other aim of the English in establishing these governments and the alliances against the Turks, was that if the Turks and Russians agreed to reactivate the 1907 convention,[99] they would have achieved a buffer zone with the Russians in the Iraqi border.

In the meantime, the English continued their activities directed against Turkey without disruptions. On the one hand they sent the Nestorians to the southern area of Hakkâri, and on the other hand, up to Badlis,[100] Gharzan and Erzurum regions, sending money and conducting propaganda, spread and strengthen the idea of independence among Kurdish tribes and especially among the Kurdish leaders in Badlis and adversaries around Erzurum. So much so that the most effective [propaganda] reached Turkish officers and got hold of some officers; in this manner they wanted to weaken the Turks on the Mosul question and even going too far to take over Turkey's eastern and southeastern sections.

The Turkish Government saw all these types of secret activities that

---

98. Kurdish tribal leader Sıdda was an ally of the Assyrians.
99. The Anglo-Russian Entente or the Anglo-Russian Convention of 1907.
100. Bitlis today.

surfaced. To counteract their operations, at the end of June 1924 it decided to spread propaganda outside the *status quo* borders by forming a special organisation composed of the tribes and increase propaganda activities within the Mosul province. The aim of the Turks in taking counter measures was to break the arm of the English, which was extended to Hakkâri by using the Nestorians, and at the same time when the Mosul question was discussed at the League of Nations, to get rid of the Nestorians by way of occupation of their places and to ensure controlling circumstances in the Mosul negotiations, because the English asserted that the southern section of the borders identified at the Halich Conference belonged to Iraq (the border which follows River Hazil which passes through the immediate north of the towns of Shemsdinan, Julamerk, Beyt-Shebab [Beyt-Shewawe], and reaches the Euphrates).

THE UPRISING

The situation before the uprising

The decision of the Turkish Government to engage in propaganda activities over the border to counteract the English provocation, was firstly an issue of organisation. To bring forth such an organisation, to prevent the English from using the Nestorians to spread propaganda among the Kurds, it was first necessary to disarm the Nestorians within the Turkish borders, who were armed by the English. If such an operation was undertaken, even if the English did not get involved, the Nestorians within the Turkish borders would, either after a short resistance, have gone over the border, or, have resisted in the areas they still lived with the support of their brethren outside the borders, who had a regular organisation. Yet, in this part of the region (the region in the east of River Hazil which forms the southern border of the Silopi sub-district of Gziro [Gezira][101] and the south of Julamerk), the Turkish Government had neither an organisation nor a military force. It was first necessary to send soldiers to this region and [set up] an administrative organisation. For this purpose, it was necessary to send an infantry regiment and a mountain artillery battery to Beyt-Shebab and an infantry battalion and a mountain team to Julamerk.

It was also necessary to benefit from the Kurdish tribes in the organisation to be formed, with the aim of counteracting the destructive propaganda. Even though some tribes seemed to be in favour in the beginning, they could not be trusted much. Nonetheless, it was thought that if their leaders, who in general had criminal records, would help if they did not fear the Turkish soldiers who would approach the region. As for the operation, these tribes could have been assigned under the command of the detachment commanders in their areas, and by paying attention to the situation and of the tribal peculiarities it could have been possible to benefit from them to the maximum degree.

In order to prevent the return of the Nestorians, having been driven across the border after a short resistance, as the battalions in this region were not sufficient, it was also necessary to form a border battalion in

---
101. Also known as Jaziret ibn-'Omar, Jazire; Cizre in Turkish.

the space between Gziro and Julamerk, especially in the part belonging to the Nestorians. The factor which forced the Turkish Government to take this type of measures to ensure security were various and quite serious. The armed Nestorians who were assembling in the Hakkâri region, through the provocation and incitement by the English, were increasing their safety and order, destroying operations, a little more every day.

The Hangediği Incident (uprising)

Finally, one day (17 August 1924) they wounded and captured the Governor of Hakkâri around Hangediği and they martyred the gendarme commander and a few soldiers. The Governor Halil Rıfat Bey described the uprising which *de facto* began in this manner, as follows:

> "We set out from Julamerk to Chal on 7 August 1924 to see the special organisation of the tribes of Chal after Beyt-Shebab, the Nestorian position and forces, and, carry out some other important tasks. The Province Gendarme Commander who went out to inspect, the gendarme lieutenant appointed to Chal, nine infantry men, six cavalry gendarme men, a tax collector, four unarmed civilians, three of them animal renters, were with us. Despite all the measures taken not to come into contact with the Nestorians, our path was crossing in the easternmost point of the Nestorian borders, seven hours away from the southern tribe, by the creek where there were only five-six houses. In the early hours of the next morning crossing this creek, suddenly we came under crossfire from four directions. When it was understood that a governor was among the passengers they stopped firing and surrounded us. That day on which we became captives and the arms and ammunition of the surviving gendarmes were taken, we were taken to a distance eight hours away, to the leader of the Nuhub [Tuxub, Txuma] tribe and the organiser of this murderous incident; someone by the name Gulyano."

> "Next day, we were set out on our way in order to be handed over to the Iraqi 'Amadiye Government. The guards may have received English military training such that they behaved exactly like the English. When we arrived to the village Kiman belonging to the Lower Tiyyari, a person by the name Khoshaba, who despite being one of the most powerful of the Lower Tiyyari Nestorians has always proved to our government to be a friend, tried to prevent the situation. Despite the obstinacy of the guards, he informed them that he would resist by force. A day later he used the same force against Gulyano, who came there, and restored our liberty. Today we came to Chal. In this skirmish the Province Gendarme Commander Major Hüseyin and three gendarmes became martyrs and five of our gendarme soldiers were wounded - three of them seriously."

The reason for the incident: the murderers were claiming that some of the tribes in Chal and its environs were asking the government to send soldiers upon them. Naturally they found out about our operation and one day earlier took measures and committed this murder on purpose. When we were in Nuhub [Tuxub] with Gulyano, two English planes flew above us, and in the morning in a quite low [altitude] two airplanes hovered around within our borders and their wish to send us to 'Amadiye as captives and the appearance of uniformed and armed English soldiers among the Nestorians, leaves no doubt that the English lately are inciting these murderers against our government. This very distressing journey and incident demonstrated to us that the places where the Nestorians are located consist of difficult to pass through high mountains, impossible to walk on with shoes, deep creeks, places with no roads and uninhabited. If a military operation is to be undertaken it demonstrate to us the definite need of the commander to personally inspect this area and that if they did not receive assistance from the south their force to be composed of no less than 2,000 good marksmen.

Although this incident caused me to shed bloody tears, it gave a good reason to our government to suppress the Nestorians and throw them out of their land.

SUPPRESSION OPERATION

Thoughts on the necessity of the operation of suppression and prior measures taken:

This incident had rendered the punishment of the Nestorians bandits who rebelled, an absolute necessity. However, the operation to be organized to suppress this uprising needed to be undertaken with calm and foresight and to rely on a foundation of achievement of success by taking all the requisite measure and with little force.

In reality, because this incident occurred by outside influence and inculcation and expanded even more to take on a political dimension, there was a possibility of creating a great danger.

The measures taken with this consideration, needed to be sufficient to an extent that in the event that the Nestorians over the border participated in the uprising, would have enabled an irrevocable operation against all of them, at the same time. As the problem necessitated preparation, speed, severity and irrevocability, it was necessary not to be reluctant on expenses *etc*. Otherwise, the time that would have been lost would have been in favour of the insurgents, as well as have a bad effect on the region's public opinion and would have made the operation harder.

The commander of the 7th Army Corps who saw the seriousness and precariousness of the situation, since the English were supporting the Nestorians mentally and materially, he thought it was possible to start the operation in a definite manner after a thorough preparation and address the inexperience of the soldiers by increasing their numbers, and at the same time benefit from the tribes to an absolute degree. In order to achieve this, he saw it appropriate to give gifts and money to tribal chiefs and for the government to reward them by medallions.

As for the General Staff Command, due to the gravity of the situation in order to set aside sufficient forces on 12 August 1924, ordered the 9th Army Corps to send a regiment from the 12th Division to Van and they reserved the 36th Regiment for this duty.

Additionally, the General Staff Command, on the same day (12th of August) told the 7th Army Corps that it was decided to punish the Nestorian bandits who ambushed the Governor of Van by force and if other Nestorians resisted to get rid of them completely from within our borders and asked what sort of measures needed to be taken for the operation to end fast and with complete success and informed that for this reason 40,000 liras were sent to the Army Corps.

According to the 7th Army Corps' thoughts for the operation, firstly to make the detachments mobile, the procurement of vehicles and provisions was necessary. Because only with this possibility it was necessary to use force [sic].

The Chief of General Staff who received the consideration of the 3rd Army Inspector and the 7th Army Corps Commander, on this matter concerning the operation which was decided to be undertaken, on 13 August 1924 presented his thoughts to the Office of the Prime Minister as follows:

1. The area in which the Nestorians to be suppressed is located at:

-The line its north of which lies between the south of Beyt-Shebab and south of Julamerk;

-Its east between Oramar and Chal's western borders;

-Its south, south of 'Amadiye;

-Its west, an area which is a difficult to pass and borders with the Galliya-Goyan tribes and Mount Neri-Nar. The population is about 8,000 and we have been informed that about 1,000 [of them] will be armed. The people under suppression may take the following steps:

a) Without using arms against the suppression forces, they may leave their homes and emigrate to the south.

b) They may resist without any outside help.

c) They may resist contented with the help of their friend around the region (Zakho, 'Amadiye, 'Aqra, Zibar and Rewanduz) with an orderly organisation, as we have learned, composed of five battalions, 600-strong each.

d) They may be helped with arms belonging to the flock of people gathered around Urmia.

e) To strengthen the resistance of the insurgents, the English forces in Mosul and its environs may participate in the operation.

2. Among the specified operational options the possibility of the Nestorians emigrating or resisting on their own are remote. Likewise, as the *de facto* participation of the English would mean a declaration of war between the Turkish Government and English Government, this is not considered likely. For this reason the strongest possibility

may be thought to be the likelihood of the organized Nestorians in the region, from near the borders, to meddle in the Nestorians in our country or help them to resist. In this case, in order to deal a decisive blow to this mass in a short period of time it is seen appropriate to conduct an operation with the 2nd Infantry and 1st Cavalry Divisions and take the following measures [by sending]:

a) the 1st Infantry Regiment of the 2nd Infantry Division in Van and a mountain artillery battery to Julamerk;

b) the 18th Regiment in Shirnakh[102] to Beyt-Shebab;

c) the 6th Regiment in Midyat and one of the artillery batteries around Gziro to Hadrish (10 km southwest of Beyt-Shebab);

d) the 1st Cavalry Division around Gziro to the area between Gziro and Hadrish (because the terrain is rough, if no benefit comes from the use of the Cavalry Division, then the use of 17th Division forces is being considered);

e) one regiment from the 12th Infantry Division in Sarikamish and a mountain artillery battery to Van;

f) the 5th Regiment of the 14th Cavalry Division in Mardin, the Cavalry Squadron of the 7th Army Corps in Nsibin and an infantry battalion from the 17th Division in Omid and two artillery shells from the 2nd Artillery Division and a field artillery battery from the 7th Army Corps to Gziro;

g) from the air forces in Smyrna [Izmir], a squadron of eight airplanes to Mardin;

h) the forward echelon of the Headquarters of the 7th Army Corps, which is to manage the operation, to Gziro and to appoint the 2nd Division Commander Major General Kâzım Pasha, who was appointed to the Badlis governorate, to head the division;

3. Since it will not be possible to procure provisions in the Nestorian region when the operation will be carried out, the tasks specified in the second clause, may be undertaken after the arrival of provisions and ammunition to Julamerk, Beyt-Shebab, Hadrish and southern regions and the airplane squadron to Mardin.

4. After the procurement of provisions and ammunition and completion of the airplanes' flight preparation, the forces will move from their position and the Kurdish tribes from Julamerk, Beyt-Shebab, Galliya-Goyan, Shirnakh and Gziro regions which will be secured

---

102. Şırnak in Turkish.

with monetary sacrifices, under the command of their own leaders and by giving to the employ of these leaders officers who know the peculiarities of the region and trustworthy in every respect, attack the Nestorian region with small detachments, while the forces will follow them as auxiliary forces.

It is thought that the operation should start by entering Beyt-Shebab and Hadrish with the forces from the south, northwest and west of the region where Nestorians are located.

5. The reason for bringing an infantry regiment to Van is to shield and protect Van and Hakkâri provinces from possible attack that may occur on the Iranian border. The reason for bringing the forces to the environs of Gziro is to counteract a possible attack that may occur in the Zakho region.

6. With the proviso of ensuring him to work in our favour in the Khoy/Urmia regions, at this point, it is considered to be appropriate to send Simko against the Nestorians and Armenians who are expected to become active in the Shemsdinan region and Iran.

7. It is considered appropriate to station a gendarme battalion around Badlis and gendarmes in the Iranian border and increase our forces with the participation of the gendarme of the Van Border Battalion to the operation.

8. If these measures are approved by your office, I petition you to give the necessary order to start preparations and the operation.

Ministerial Council's decision concerning the suppression of the uprising

Upon the Chief of General Staff's proposal, the Ministerial Council took the following decision to suppress the uprising (summary):

"The measures to be taken against Nestorians due to the Hangediği incident in the Hakkâri province, were discussed in the Ministerial Council meeting of 14 August 1924, and it was decided to inform the relevant ministries to carry out and follow up these matters:

1. The General Staff Command has been assigned to suppress the Nestorian uprising. Nestorians caught with arms will be punished absolutely. By a separate decision, necessary appropriations have been arranged.

2. Other than the ideas and measures of the General Staff Command which we were informed about, to bring also a regiment to the Badlis region and not to count the Badlis Mobile Gendarme Battalion as participators to the operation and the Van Gendarme Battalion to be transferred only after the arrival of said regiment.

3. To carry out the operation as fast as possible and not to violate the *status quo* borders. The measures proposed by the General Staff concerning the use of the tribes and Simko has been considered appropriate.

4. It is being been considered not to remove the Governor of Badlis from Badlis."

Operation preparations

From the point of view of strengthening the influence of the state on the tribes, the operation related to domestic policies, while from the point of view of the Mosul question, which was about to be resolved, related to foreign policies. Accordingly, it needed to conclude successfully, commensurate with its importance, come what may.

On the same day (14 August 1924) of the Ministerial Council's decision concerning the suppression of the Nestorian uprising, the General Staff Command as initial measures ordered these organisational and deployment changes:

In the 7th Army Corps:	the 1st Battalion of the 17th Division in Omid to Shirnakh; the regimental headquarters in Ma´murat ul-´Aziz [Elazığ], with its 2nd Battalion to Omid; the 63rd Regiment in Malatya to Ma´murat ul-´Aziz; the 17th Division Commander Nurettin Pasha temporarily to leave his division to the brigade commander and in order to manage the 2nd Division Command [to transfer] to the 2nd Division; the Cavalry Squadron of the 7th Army Corps and the 5th Cavalry Regiment of the 14th Cavalry Division in Mardin to the Gziro region.

In the 9th Army Corps:	one infantry regiment of the 9th Division and a mountain artillery battery to Van; an infantry regiment of the 12th Division which was prepared to go to Van and a mountain artillery battery to be sent to Badlis and when these detachments arrive to their regions to be assigned under the command of the 7th Army Corps.

The General Staff Command, moreover, in an order published on 16 August 1924 [stated]:

-Upon the request of the 7th Army Corps Commander, all infantry forces of the 2nd Infantry Division and two heavy mountain artillery batteries and the 1st Cavalry Division to participate entirely in the operation;

-Other than these, the forces which were seen necessary to participate in the operation, to operate according to the order issued on the 14th of August regarding the deployment changes;

-If necessary, propose the increase of the 2nd Division artillerymen;

-Due to the participation in the operation of an 8-airplane squadron from the air force, to send immediately the airplane expert of the 3rd Army Inspectorate to Omid under the command of the 7th Army Corps; also to prepare airstrips of 1 km² in the north of Mardin and much smaller around Gziro, as soon as possible;

-The 7th Army Corps Commander to direct the operation personally;

-In order to protect communication between the forces which were assigned to the operation and sent from different directions, three mountain radiotelephone centres, from the 1st, 3rd and 9th Divisions were requested from the Defense Ministry to be sent immediately to Diyarbakır, under the command of the 7th Army Corps.

Around this time, the General Staff Command, from a report it received from the Iran Border Station, learned that some Nestorians from Iran and another Nestorian force and the tribal forces secured by Sıdda, would attack Shemsdinan from the Rewanduz direction and another force from the direction of Chal, by marching to Julamerk, would occupy Hakkâri. In order to ensure that the border battalions are not destroyed bit by bit, the General Staff Command ordered the Julamerk Border battalion to station in an appropriate place to counteract possible raids that may occur from the directions of Rewanduz and Shemsdinan. Likewise, it was ordered that the Van Border Battalion to leave its observation service to the fixed gendarme and moreover that these battalions to be assigned under the command of the 7th Army Corps.

The report received from the 7th Army Corps on 17th of August informed that:

-The 6th Regiment to move from Midyat to Shirnakh in six days:

-The 1st Battalion of the 62nd Regiment departed from Omid on the 20th of August and arrived in Shirnakh on the 4th of September;

-The 62nd Regimental Headquarters and the 2nd Battalion departed on the 19th of August from Ma'murat ul-'Aziz to arrive in Omid on the 24th of August;

-The 63rd Regiment departed from Malatya on the 19th of August to arrive in Ma'murat ul-'Aziz in four stops;

-The Infantry Squadron of the 7th Army Corps and the 5th Cavalry Regiment to set out for Gziro once sufficient provisions procured;

-The 18th Regiment to Beyt-Shebab;

-The 6th Regiment to be sent to Hadrish; likewise it has been ordered that the 1st Regiment in Van to set out to Julamerk with an artillery battery, in order to go to 'Albaq [Başkale];

-The 17th Division Commander Nurettin Pasha to set out from Ma'murat ul-'Aziz for Sa'irt[103] on the 20th of August;

-To start reconnaissance and preparations for the air fields in Mardin and Gziro.

The order of General Staff Command gave to the 7th Army Corps on the 18th of August [was]:

The participation in the operation of other than two more mountain artillery batteries and the entire 1st Cavalry Division, the 2nd Infantry Division and two heavy mountain artillery batteries and the 1st Cavalry Division. Likewise, the 2nd Battalion of the 62nd Regiment due to arrive in Omid and the Regimental Headquarters, to be taken to Mardin and a field artillery battery from Omid and 2nd Division artillery shell to around Gziro. One battalion from the 63rd Regiment, which is in Ma'murat ul-'Aziz, to be taken to Omid. Also, to gather 1,000 tribal soldiers in Julamerk, 400 in Beyt-Shebab, 800 in Harbol, 400 in Gziro; the Van Border Battalion and one artillery battery from the regiment due to arrive to Van, as a group to 'Albaq and surroundings. The Army Corps proposal to station Julamerk

---

103. Siirt in Turkish.

Border Battalion in Gewar and Shemsdinan against Iran, has been found appropriate and ordered the following organisation envisaged for the forces in the area in which the operations is to be carried out:

The Bashkale Group:

Its commander:	Van Governor and South East Border Police Chief, 8th Tribal Division Commander, Colonel Süleyman Sabri
Its detachments:	9th Division Headquarters 28th Infantry Regiment of the 9th Division A group of mountain artillery batteries from the 9th Division 5th Van Border Battalion 6th Julamerk Border Battalion (on the 27th of September it was placed under the command of the Julamerk Group) Parts of the 8th Tribal Division (those that could be gathered)

The Julamerk Group:

Its commander:	Commander of the 1st Regiment of the 2nd Division, Lieutenant Colonel Osman ´Avni
Its detachments:	1st Infantry Regiment A heavy mountain artillery battery from the 2nd Division artillerymen 1,000 tribal soldiers A mountain radiotelephone centre (from the 9th Division)

The Beyt-Shebab Group:

Its commander:	Commander of the 17th Division. Major General Nurettin Pasha

Its detachments:	The 6th Regiment of the 2nd Division The 18th Regiment of the 2nd Division Two powerful Krupp mountain artillery batteries from the 2nd Division artillerymen A cavalry squadron 400 tribal soldiers A mountain radiotelephone centre

The Khabur Group:

Its commander:	Commander of the 1st Cavalry Division. Major General Mürsel Pasha
Its detachments:	1st Cavalry Division (11th, 14th, 21st Cavalry Regiments, a mountain artillery battery) 800 tribal soldiers A mountain radiotelephone centre

The Gziro Group:

Its commander:	Commander of the 14th Cavalry Division Brigadier Ferit Bey
Its detachments:	5th Cavalry Regiment of the 14th Cavalry Division A field artillery battery A mountain artillery battery 400 tribal soldiers

Units belonging to the 7th Army Corps:

	1st Battalion of the 62nd Regiment of the 17th Division
	7th Army Corps Cavalry Squadron

In order to prepare the detachments which were to participate in the operation, there was a need for sufficient funds. The Ministerial Council, which saw this need, appropriated two hundred and fifty thousand liras for the operation. Due financial formalities [red tape], the money could only be transferred on 18 August 1924 and the 7th Army Corps did not have any money in its cashier's office to take the payment. As this situation related to the preparations, it would have caused delays to the operation. The prompt beginning of the operation was dependent on the completion of the preparation as soon as possible. In this regard, on the 21st of August the General Staff requested from the Office of the Prime Minister the money to be sent promptly and give the necessary importance and speed to the work on this matter, which related to the domestic and external policies of the country.

Whilst the military preparations were under way, it was required to speed up the propaganda and insist upon inculcation of the following matter:

"The Nestorian bandits who captured the governor of Hakkâri and wounded and martyred our gendarmes and the tribes and people who help them will be severely routed no matter what. These nobodies will be pursued even if they leave for Mosul, or even for England. Those who do not use arms against our soldiers will most certainly not be fired upon. Moreover, those who earlier did not obey the government, in the event that they take refuge with us, will be treated well. Even Sıdda, if he takes refuge and obeys [us] he will be treated in the same manner."

In this manner, by spreading fear and wavering among the tribes, the reduction of the effect of the propaganda spread by the English side, which wanted to create defeatism and opposition, was sought.

According to the views of the Commander of the 7th Army Corps, Ja´fer Tayyar Pasha, who was in charge of the suppression operation, in a report presented to the Chief of Staff Command on 23 August 1924 concerning the situation of the detachments on the operations' administration [stated]:

"Most of the soldiers were new and among them there was no one who participated in a battle. One third of the extant [forces] composed of supply soldiers who transferred to the detachments within the last two months. As part of the forces moved towards the areas of assembly, in accordance to prior orders, this meant that their training was stopped - at least partly. In this regard, in order to make them solid, it was necessary to start training immediately in the assembly areas; within one or two days to complete lessons and combat shooting and get them used to mountain battles."

It was possible to get rid of the Nestorians bandits with the forces extant within the borders of Hakkâri. Nonetheless, as these [people] were reinforced from Mosul and just as our Rumeli/Montenegro border was controlled by the Austrian General Staff, here, if the Nestorians were ruled, protected and supported by the English, the speedy resolution of the matter would have become quite hard.

For this reason, it would be a prudent measure to wait completely for the detachments, which were given the duty to carry out the operation, to arrive in the assembly areas, and secure the supply and ammunition situation. With this consideration, before embarking upon the decisive suppression operation, the Army Corps needed to organise the following matters:

-to arrange the supply and battle matters thoroughly;

-to amass sufficient ammunition in the operation area;

-to disseminate propaganda widely, in order to facilitate the participation of a great number of tribes in our operation;

-to start the operation for certain in the beginning of September, in order to complete the operation by mid-October when the season in the region is not suitable.

As the assemblage of the cavalry division would generally be dependent on the situation of the Galliya-Goyan tribe, to benefit from them in the event that this tribe joins the operation on our behalf. If they remain neutral, the cavalry division to transfer to the area between Rumni and Challek Bridge on River Khabur.[104] Although it is not expected, if the tribe operate against us, to leave the cavalry division in Harbol and Bespin regions. In this situation, the 1st Battalion of the 62nd Regiment which is to come to Shirnakh and the 2nd Battalion of the 62nd Regiment which is to come to Mardin and the Army Corps Cavalry squadron to be used in the duty assigned to the cavalry division. In this eventuality, to utilise the cavalry division in accordance to the development of the situation and in the meantime to get this division to do field reconnaissance for various objectives.

Gziro Border Battalion to leave its duty in near Tigris and assemble in the east of Gziro.

No matter how, the 28th Infantry Regiment and the mountain artillery battery, due to arrive to Van, is to be stationed in ʹAlbaq as a group. It was appropriate the 63rd Regiment due to arrive to Badlis and the mountain artillery battery due to arrive to their [designated] places and the 63rd Regiment to be taken to Mardin. After the assemblage is completed in this manner, the groups which during the conduct of the operation would separate by big distances in the Nestorian high plateau to continue their operation relying on controlling positions.

The Julamerk group [to go] over the line separating Dar ul-Tawbe and Beylan, to a position controlling River Zab Valley.

The Beyt-Shebab group [to go] either to Diyari-zor mountain pass or to the Nestorian high plateau's upper part line over Zel-Shirski.

The Khabur group, which will come into existence through the 1st or the 2nd Battalion of the 62nd Regiment with Army Corps Cavalry Squadron, is appropriate to be directed to the Develi mountain ridges controlling Lower Tiyyari.

---

104. Habur Suyu in Turkish, Nahr al Khabur in Arabic.

In this manner, after our detachments arrive to controlling parts of the Nestorian high plateau, between Rivers Zab and Khabur, it is possible that the Nestorians whose most of the villages are in the valleys, may retreat to the south or towards the east of Sıdda's possible operation area. If that happened, the continuation of the operation would be dependent on the measures to be undertaken.

During the operation it would be more appropriate for Van Border Battalion to be assigned under the command of the ʹAlbaq Group and Julamerk Border Battalion to spy on the Sıdda force in Shemsdinan region and counteract, and be utilised under the command of the Julamerk Group Commander.

Although the General Staff Command found appropriate the 7th Army Corps' thoughts on the operation, felt the need to warn the army corps on these matters on 26 August 1924:

According to the Chief of General Staff Fevzi Chakmak [Çakmak] Pasha, the Nestorian forces within our border have 1,000 – 3,000 rifles. Those Nestorian infantry detachments outside our borders, about which we learned that previously they were cavalries in Arbil and Mosul, in total they are seven-eight battalions with 300-600 extant [soldiers]. If you add these to the Nestorian forces within our border, it needs to be accepted that the total will increase to 3,400, at most to 7,500, extant riffles.

As the Province of Hakkâri belonged to the Republic of Turkey, in accordance to the domestic *status quo*, it was not possible for people who lived within these borders to have artillery and airplanes. At the very most, they could have had some machine guns. With this consideration it was absolutely possible to rout the rebellious Nestorians by including artillery, machine guns and especially airplanes in the operation, to destroy their morale. In the event that the Nestorians held artilleries and airplanes they would have naturally belonged to the English. This would have meant England declaring war against the Turkish Government, such that at that time something like that would not have been considered [by the English]. If it did, there would have been no reason to maintain the *status quo* and it would have constituted a reason to continue the attack over to Mosul.

The strongest evidence that the Nestorian forces were no more than ten battalions and at most a few thousand individuals was that, a detachment consisting of three battalions participated in the operation carried out by Sir Salmon. Likewise, it was also a fact that Özdemir Bey, with a few hundred soldiers and the assistance of Kurds routed thousands of Nestorians. The English, as they always do, would spread an exaggerated propaganda among the tribes, within the army corps, the province, even in Ankara, and personally to the Chief of General

Staff, about the ampleness of their forces, that our operation would not succeed. It was necessary to take into account this among the measures to be taken and spread that we would attack with four divisions and a total of 40,000 people.

The arrival of the regiment, which was found appropriate to arrive in Van and kept at ʿAlbaq, was not to affect the operation. Although now there were sufficient forces in Badlis, the 36th Regiment and the mountain artillery battery was also on its way to Badlis.

During the suppression operation, the Beyt-Shebab and Khabur Groups were in close proximity to each other and if necessary there was the possibility of intervening; they could be directed as required. Since it was possible that during the operation the radiotelephone may have become silent, the Commander of the 1st Regiment, who was responsible for the command of the Julamerk Border Battalion to be stationed in Shemsdinan, might have been forced to operate on his own, without any orders, it was necessary to give detailed instructions to this group, clearly explaining the aim and intention.

Rumours to the effect that some Nestorians were in favour of the Government of the Republic and that they would help the Governor Halil Rıfat Bey, ought not to be trusted and in any case we should have been alert to a high degree. It should have been even taken into consideration that some Kurds would have fooled by the English, and we should have inspired confidence to the likes of them. In the meantime, the matter of procurement most necessary for the operation was being followed up with importance. Finally, on 26 August, a total of 100,000 liras, composed of 50,000 from the Omid Ottoman Bank, 30,000 from the Ziraat Bank and 20,000 from the office of the director of finance, were supplied, and moreover the Ottoman Bank granted 200,000 liras of credit for the use of the Army Corps. Consequently, the lack of funds, which prevented the starting of the operation, was alleviated. For this reason, the General Staff ordered the army corps to identify the date of the start of the operation and inform them.

The General Staff Command in order to clarify further the measures that were being taken and to be undertaken, in the command issued to the 7th Army Corps Command on 27 August 1924 [stated]: "it is not considered probable at the moment the *de facto* meddling of the English during the operation to be conducted in Hakkâri province. Yet, it would be foresighted to accept that the English as always, by resorting to the use of a variety of means and games, will encourage the Armenians and Nestorians in Urmia and the Iranians from the east, the Nestorians and the other Arabs and the tribes from the south (from Gziro region), the Kurds in Badlis and its environs from within, to attack and make attempts to bolster the events around the borders by flying airplanes.

In order to counteract the assaults, which were possible to come from the Iranian region, the ʹAlbaq Group and the 7th Tribal Division, in the region of Beyazıt against the resistances in the Hakkâri regions, detachments to be gathered from this region, for the insurgence in the environs of Badlis forces to come from the 9th Army Corps, [and] for the Bedouin Arabs' attacks which had the possibility of eventuating in Gziro, Nsibin and Mardin regions, it would have been appropriate to reinforce the organisation established. With this aim it would have been a prudent measure to spread around propaganda that the regiments of the 14th Cavalry Division which were in ʹAyntab[105] and Urhoy and the division headquarters were to transfer temporarily around Mardin and that from these forces two squadrons were to be sent to Nsibin and that by attacking from that area Mosul would be taken back.

In the event that the commander of the 7th Army Corps, in order to personally direct the operation, became distant from the region, then Gziro and Mardin groups were to be left to the command of the division commander and in order to protect more thoroughly the communication between his headquarters and the General Staff, it would have made things easier if the Commander of the 14th Cavalry Division Colonel Suphi was brought to Gziro immediately and assigned for the duty.

The preparations underway were progressing despite the difficulties encountered and in the meantime the situation of the other side was being monitored closely.

On 31 August 1924, the 7th Army Corps, relying on information received from the Hakkâri Province, in a report submitted to the General Staff Command, stated: "the possibility of English airplanes and the Nestorians who compose their detachments in Iraq, crossing the border and helping the Nestorians in our place is certain. In order to prevent this, it is necessary that Ankara makes attempt [to formulate] new policies as soon as possible."

The thought and opinion of the General Staff Command on this news was:

"The matter does not necessitate entering into new political efforts; on the contrary, it necessitates the opposite. The English by applying to the League of Nation claimed the necessity to leave to Iraq the south of the fictive line passing through Julamerk and Beyt-Shebab. In reply, our wish was to station our forces in the southern border of the Hakkâri Province, which is still regarded as the theoretical border. Since the Lausanne Treaty was signed by governments, it is imperative for the Turkish Republic to add the Mosul question to the negotiations in the League of Nations in twenty days. Consequently, before the expiry of

---

105. Antep in Turkish, today Gaziantep.

this period it was necessary to achieve a victory. Otherwise to change the decision the League of Nations would take against us, or to undertake an operation contrary to its judgement would undoubtedly lead to great political difficulties. With this consideration, it was necessary to determine the beginning and the conclusion of the operation. Furthermore, it was important to strengthen and speed up intelligence and continue propaganda and spread [rumours] to the effect that the English do not have any detachments in Iraq, only that they appear with their airplanes trying to affect morale and that because the Nestorian detachments wore English clothes the impression that the English were in Iraq was completely wrong and secure a large number of tribes to participate in the operation in a useful way."

The detachments were continuing to approach their areas of assembly in accordance to earlier orders. In the meantime, on 3 September 1924, the General Staff Command seeing the need, it ordered the 7th Army Corps to send the 14th Cavalry Division Headquarters and the 3rd Regiment of this division from Urhoy [Edessa, Urfa] to Mardin, the 54th Regiment from ʹAyntab to Urhoy and, if necessary, the regiment artillerymen to Mardin.

Because the situation necessitated the preparations to be completed fast, and as soon as possible, so as to start the operation, division commands were asked whether or not there was the possibility to start in August at the latest. In the responses received, there were two main hurdles identified which prevented the speeding up of the operation. The first was the lack of available sufficient food-supplies in the region and the second the inability to procure sufficient [number of] transportation vehicles for the procurement of supplies to reach the detachments. Despite all the efforts it was estimated that the detachments would reach their destinations on the following dates:

The Julamerk Group:	In Julamerk on 3-4 September 1924
The Beyt-Shebab Group:	In Beyt-Shebab on 2-3 September 1924
The 6th Regiment:	In Hadrish, on 6-7 September 1924
The 1st Cavalry Division	In Badlis, on 3-4 September 1924
The 5th Cavalry Regiment and two mountain artillery batteries:	In Gziro, on 3-4 September 1924

The 36th Regiment and one mountain artillery battery:	In Badlis, on 8-10 September 1924
The 28th Regiment and one mountain artillery battery:	In Van, on 15 September 1924
The 1st Army Corps radiotelephone:	In Gziro, on 9-10 September 1924
The 3rd Army Corps radiotelephone:	In Gziro, on 10-11 September 1924
The 9th Army Corps radiotelephone:	In Van, on 9-10 September 1924
Airplanes:	In Mardin and Gziro, on 10-15 September.

In this situation, arrival to the assembly areas would have been possible by the 15th of September. Since it was necessary for the operation not be delayed, efforts were made to assemble the 2nd Division units and the 1st Cavalry Division rapidly and procure the requisite provisions and munitions. Nonetheless, if the operation started only with them, it would not have been possible for the radio telegraphs necessary for communication and the airplanes to participate in the operation. In the meantime, the tribal soldiers who were to participate in the operation were informed to assemble in the designated places and positive response was received.

The General Staff Command which was preparing the suppression operation was also considering the propaganda activities with the aim of destroying the morale of the other side and to boost the morale of our officers, the tribal leaders and our soldiers. In an order it given to the 7th Army Corps on 6 September 1924, it was pointed out that:

"It is requested that the news that a regiment from each of the 9th, 6th and the 5th Army Corpses and a mountain artillery battery be sent rapidly to the Badlis and Gziro Regions, that other than the airplane squadron which is about to arrive in Mardin, another airplane squadron is about to depart and that the government absolutely wants our military force to occupy the region up to the southern border of Hakkâri; that the outcome will be achieved by destroying any hurdles that will oppose this. For this propaganda to be effective it is seen as important to identify henceforth temporary encampments in Badlis and Gziro regions. Furthermore, it is also required to spread extensively the matter that the operation is not about suppressing all the Nestorians but only the aim being the punishment of the gang which occupied the southern border of the Hakkâri Province and attacked the Governor of Hakkâri. Every person who acts against our soldiers with good will and does not fire a weapon, will - without distinction - be treated well and the gang to be caught will be handed over to justice. Not even a minor harm will come to the other people who obey. In order to keep our troops' morale high we will need to explain the matter to our soldiers in a convincing manner: that those who will want to oppose them do not have a regular organisation and forces; that they are waylays; that their numbers and arms are limited; that on the contrary the number of our forces who are going to thrash them severely is high and equipped with airplanes, artillery and machine guns."

Benefiting from the tribes

Upon the decision of the Ministerial Council concerning the suppression of the Nestorian Uprising, the General Staff Command on the 16th of August asked the South East Border Station and the 7th Army Corps Command, in which places was it possible to make use of the Kurdish tribe Shikak leader Sheikh[106] İsmail Agha (Simko), who was in Turkey as refugee, and for that, what was needed to be done; moreover, in what way could make use of the tribes in Shemsdinan, Gewar (Yüksekova), 'Albaq and Saray regions and whether it would be more appropriate to use them against the Nestorians or to have them assembled *en masse* around the Iranian border. According to the thoughts of both authorities: with the proviso of being under the command of the 8th Tribal Division, it was appropriate to have Simko first in the 'Albaq region to use him against the Armenians in Tergewar and Mergewar regions.

This way [to prevent] the Armenians from making the Nestorian operation difficult, and facilitating Sıdda's possible attacks on Shemsdinan and against the possibility that they may attack Hakkâri from the south, a mass force would have been at hand. Nonetheless, the use of Simko for this aim was dependent on compensation, even partially, for the financial damage he suffered when he sought refuge in Turkey. It was also necessary to make efforts to benefit from the tribes in Shemsdinan and Gewar regions, whose morale in the recent Rewanduz issue was shaken, although a large part of the tribes due to friendship and relation ties were loyal to and admired Sıdda. As for the tribes in 'Albaq and Saray regions especially, since they did not have connection with the south,

---

106. *Şeyh* in Turkish.

it was necessary to use them by organising them. It was useful to use all these tribes only against a possible attack by the Iranian Armenians. For this reason, some matters such as the procurement of provisions for the tribes to participate in the operation, appropriate rewards from the discretionary fund and the grant of robs of honour, binoculars etc has been taken into consideration.

Other than these [measures] the matter of the settlement of Simko's tribe in the ́Albaq district in eleven abandoned villages and compensation for the financial damages he incurred when he took shelter, 3,000 lira from the discretionary funds were secured.

In the meantime, in order to break the morale of the other side, as well as bringing the 9th Army Corps Cavalry Squadron to Karaköse, while sending the Tribal Division Commander Hajji Arif Bey with his Headquarters to Beyazıt rapidly, the following measures of propaganda were taken: "the division of Hajji Arif Bey who with a masterly maneuver captured a division of the Greeks, has arrived in Beyazıt in order to march to Iran and that together with the soldiers who were assembled in Van, against the operation of the Nestorians in Urmia, will rout Iran for showing tolerance, with the proviso of spreading [this propaganda] secretly without telling anyone; Moreover Hajji Arif Bey to call the tribal leaders nearby, with them privately and secretly this idea of his.[107]

Before starting the suppression operation, it was necessary to take into consideration the situation of the Galliya-Goyan tribe, because at that time there were many rumours about this tribe. At the same time being prudent about this nomadic tribe, which the English made efforts to gain, it was necessary to give them all kinds of guarantees to align them to our national aim, [as] they might have used arms against the Turkish forces thinking the suppression operation is against them. Due to these objectives, Shirnakh tribal leader Süleyman Agha, who had much influence on this tribe, was sent with his entourage under the command of the 1st Cavalry Division and moreover former Nsibin Draft Office Chief Major Sıtkı, who knew the situation of the region very well, was sent to the side of the 1st Cavalry Division Commander Mürsel Pasha with robs of honour and a number of gifts in order to give them to Galliya-Goyan tribal leader.

The aim in all these efforts was to secure this tribe and in the beginning of the operation without firing a weapon, to pass through the area they are located and to ensure their neutrality, even if they did not collaborate with us. In this regard, it was resorted to all kinds of actions. Due to the attention the government paid, Simko's ties and loyalty to

---

107. I am aware of the apparent contradiction about the concept of spreading propaganda without telling anyone. I think the Rapporteur meant to say "not to tell anyone about the plan to spread propaganda".

the Turkish Republic was ensured. On the matter of using this tribe the General Staff thought this way:

The main advantage in utilising this tribe was that during the negotiations in the League of Nations, which were to start on the 20th of September, Simko would have been *de facto* in charge of Rewanduz, and with the people there, would not recognise the English occupation. During this time, the detachments which were to participate in the operation were to arrive in the southern border of the Hakkâri province. In the meantime, because of the possibility of the Nestorians who gathered around Urmia preventing Simko form entering Rewanduz was taken into consideration, it was necessary for Simko to break immediately such an operation by the Nestorians and reach Rewanduz on the 20th or the 21st of September at the latest.

To enable Simko to carry out such an operation, it was found appropriate to give him several trustworthy officers, a doctor, 400-500 experienced soldiers, a number of telephonists and nurses from the Van and Julamerk Border Battalions. Likewise 500-600 tribal soldiers from the 8th Tribal Division and, furthermore, a commander was to be selected from Iran Border Station, to assist Simko. All soldiers under the command of Simko were to be attired in civilian clothing. It was also a condition to provide identity papers within Iran and the Rewanduz region and under no circumstance to reveal their duty. Other than these, six light machines guns and soldiers in civilian clothing with horses from the 28th Regiment, due to arrive in Van, was to be assigned under Simko's command and the matter of joining the detachments before crossing the border was thought of.

If Simko entered Rewanduz without running against the Nestorians, who, according to information obtained, assembled in Iran and if he collaborated with Sheikh Mahmut who operated against the English in Iran, he would have performed a great service. Essentially, upon the concentration of the Turkish forces in the south, it was possible that the Nestorian forces would transfer to 'Amadiye, [consequently] it would have made it easier to take back Rewanduz and by the arrival of the Turkish forces to the Hakkâri Province's southern borders, the support for Simko from a close distance would have been ensured.

Another benefit for using Simko in this way was that it would have raised the impression in the League of Nation that the operation to be carried out was more than a military operation, in that, it was carried out with national forces.

Other objectives concerning internal security

During the times when the General Staff was preoccupied with the preparation of the Hakkâri Operation, in the eastern and south-western Anatolia, in areas inhabited by tribes, as a result of internal and external provocations, there were unpleasant incidents of brigandage here and there to the point of attracting the attention of the government. It was imperative for these incidents, which troubled the people of the region and the public opinion, to be prevented by the authorities. For this reason, the 2nd Division Commander, who was concurrently Badlis and Van Governor, asked the Ministry [of Internal Affairs] for the regiment and artillery battery, which was coming from Sarıkamış to Badlis, to participate in the Hakkâri operation, to be held in Malazgirt [Manzikert] to trash unmercifully the brigands in this region.

The view of the General Staff Command, which was informed of the situation through the Ministry of Internal Affairs on this matter, was that the incidents under consideration were entirely internal security issues. During the military operation to be conducted due to the Hakkâri incident, the 36th Infantry Regiment and a mountain artillery battery, which was being brought from Badlis, as well as being an element of threat against the tribes in the region, it may have been needed by the forces assigned to the suppression operation in the Hakkâri region. Since the necessity to send them to the region could have arisen, their being withheld in Malazgirt and given the task of suppression in that region would not have been right.

It was thought that during the Hakkâri suppression operation, to enter into a suppression operation which to a larger degree necessitated a military operation in the Badlis region, which formed the immediate rear, was not right. Nonetheless, it was necessary to take measures which enabled the prevention of any insurgency in the Badlis region during the operation in the south of Hakkâri, which may have arisen as a result of English provocation and influence in this region and, with force and where they are occurring, overpower minor brigandage and disobediences.

Desertion incidents among the forces

While efforts were made to suppress an uprising with the aim of ensuring the security of the country, a distressing incident appeared among the suppression operation forces and preoccupied the commandership. According to a report which reached the General Staff on 4 September 1924, Lieutenant Hurshit of Van, of the 1st Squadron of the

18th Regiment of the Beyt-Shebab Group, with his group of 76 soldiers, and a little later, Lieutenants Rasim and Tevfik, under Captain İhsan's command, with 275 soldiers, 10 automatic and 380 riffles on them, took 800 kilos wheat from the Garnakh granary and deserted towards an unknown direction.[108] According to the investigation by the Army Corps, these four officers without spreading propaganda among the soldiers, by taking a decision among themselves, deserted by ordering the soldiers [to do the same]. Yet, if the commanders of the brigades, regiments and battalions wanted, they could have prevented this situation. Even when they saw that soldiers abandoned their detachments, they did not intervene. These commanders in that situation should have used their authority as commanders. For this reason, the army corps decided to hand them over to Court Martial. Other officers were told that if they showed the same tolerance they would be laid off. Moreover, appropriate authorities were informed that pecuniary rewards would be given by General Staff to whoever caught and handed over the deserter Captain İhsan and the other officers, and if those who surrendered were from the group of deserting soldiers, they would be pardoned. In reality, some of the soldiers who were fooled by the officers and deserted, after a short while on their own, and some of them by being captured, joined their detachments.[109]

The course of events in the operation
Initial situation (8 September 1924)

The General Staff Command saw the necessity to reinforce the forces in the operation area, with a divisional headquarters, an infantry regiment, an artillery battalion headquarters and a mountain artillery battery from the 12th Division and issued the requisite order.

The situation of the forces, anxious about starting their operation as soon as possible and reach their destinations, was as follows on 8 September 1924:

12th Division Headquarters
An infantry regiment

---

108. According to the secret report compiled by İsmet Pasha the numbers of deserters was actually four officers and 400 soldiers; *Uğur Mumcu, Kürt-İslâm Ayaklanması: 1919-1925*, 26th Edition, Ankara, 2005, p. 47.
109. One deserter escaped to the British side; Anzerlioğlu, *op .cit.*, p. 146.

An artillery battalion headquarters	
A mountain artillery battery:	In Sarıkamış (ready to move to Badlis)
The 9th Army Corps Cavalry Battalion:	In Karaköse
28th Infantry Regimental Headquarters	
The 2nd Battalion of the 28th Regiment	
A mountain artillery battery	In Erjish
The 1st Battalion of the 28th Regiment	In one day distance to Erjish
Van Border battalion	In Saray-Der-'Albaq region
The 36th Infantry Regiment	
A mountain artillery battery	In Badlis
Commandership of the Julamerk Group (Commandership of the 2nd Brigade)	
An infantry regiment.	
A battery [of artillery]	In Julamerk
Julamerk Border Battalion	In Shemsdinan-Gewar-Julamerk region
Beyt-Shebab Group Commandership (2nd Division Commandership)	

The 18th Infantry Regiment	
A mountain artillery battery	
The 6th Infantry Regiment	
A mountain artillery shells battery	In Beyt-Shebab
A cavalry squadron from the 5th Cavalry Regiment	Marching to Meydani-Chavush Khabur Group Commandership (1st Cavalry Division Commandership)
The 1st Cavalry Division	In Harbul
Gziro Group Commandership (14th Cavalry Division Commandership)	
The 5th Cavalry Regiment (lacking a squadron)	
A mountain artillery battery	
A field artillery battery	
The 3rd Army Corps Radio Centre	In Gziro
The 1st Battalion of the 62nd Infantry Regiment	In Shirnakh
The 62nd Infantry Regiment Headquarter	
The 2nd Battalion of the 62nd Infantry Regiment	In Mardin (ready to move to Midyat)
The 63rd Infantry Regiment	Marching from Omid to Sa'irt

The 14th Cavalry Regiment Headquarters	
The 3rd Cavalry Regiment	
Artillery battalion	In Urhoy (ready to move to Mardin)
The 54th Cavalry Regiment	In ʿAyntab (ready to move to Urhoy)
The 1st Army Corps Mountain Radio Centre	In Nsibin (ready to move to Gziro)
The 9th Army Corps (No.4) Radio Center	In Van
The Airplane squadron	In Jerablus [Syria]
7th Army Corps Headquarters Echelon	
7th Army Corps Cavalry Squadron	
Signal Corps	In Gziro

On the same day according to the latest information the situation of the other side was thus

A battalion of 800	
A battery [of artillery]	In Zakho [Iraq]
A detachment consisting of a squadron	In Pesh-Khabur [Iraq]
A Nestorian battalion with 400 extant	In ʿAmadiye [Iraq]
A Nestorian battalion with 400 extant	In ʿAqra [Iraq]
An infantry battalion	

Two batteries	
Twenty airplanes (eight of them unusable)	In Mosul [Iraq]
A detachment of unknown size	In the Rewanduz-Suleymaniye region [Iraq]

The Chief of General Staff who was watching the developments closely and was anxious for the operation to start at as soon as possible, on 10 September 1924, according to the information he received via a telegram, the 1st Cavalry Division was to cross River Hazil[110] with a regiment and march to Shiranish; afterwards with one day intervals the other regiments were also to move and until the evening of 15 September 1924, the Cavalry Division was to assemble in River Khabur on the Bagoge-Challek bridge area and the Beyt-Shebab Group with Julamerk Group to start the operation on the 16th of September.

In the part of the Hakkâri Province which extends up to Chal (Chukurova - the part between Rivers Khabur and Zab) would have been subject to Nestorian resistance and if the English did not help, it was estimated that until the 20th of September the area between Chal and Khabur would have been be occupied.

The situation on 9 September 1924

According to the information presented by the 7th Army Corps to the General Staff Command, the situation of the groups in the operation was as follows:

The Julamerk Group: It was in Julamerk. There was nothing worthy of report regarding food supplies and health. The Group commandership purchased 200 tons of food supply items and from these, six tons via ´Albaq, ten tons via Khoshab and two tons via Van, were on their way. Reserve ammunition had not arrived yet in Julamerk. Communication between the Army Corps and the groups was handled only through the Julamerk Telegraph Office. The leader of the Ker-Avi tribe İsmail Agha had arrived in Julamerk on 6 September 1924 and reported that he was ready to serve with his entire tribe and join in when the group arrived to the ridges of the south of Lehvin, in the west of Julamerk.

The Beyt-Shebab Group: The Group Headquarters, the 6th Infan-

---
110. Hazil Suyu in Turkish, Nahr al Hazyal in Arabic.

try Regiment and a heavy mountain artillery battery were in Elki; the 18th Infantry Regiment and a Krupp mountain battalion were at 4 km of northwest of Beyt-Shebab. Due to the desertion incidents in the 1st Battalion of the 18th Regiment, the battalion formed the 1st squadron with 80 soldiers and in this way the 1st Battalion consisted of an infantry and a machine gun squadron. The deserting soldiers who joined the 2nd battalion of the 62nd Infantry Regiment, once interrogated they would join their units.

There were eight tons of food supplies in Garnakh and 20 tons in Awrahe. Furthermore, efforts were made to transport the food supplies, which were procured in a variety of places between Berwari and Beyt-Shebab, with local vehicles. The necessary food supplies for the group were procured from Badlis, Sa'irt and Gziro and on 8 September 1924, 12 tons barley and four tons of wheat were being sent from Gziro. The Groups' reserve ammunition was in Shirnakh and some ammunition was on the way to Shirnakh from Beyt-Shebab on the 3rd of September.

The communication between the Army Corps and the Group between Beyt-Shebab and Shirnakh was conducted through mounted signal corps posts and from there to Gziro through telegraph.

Signal lamp posts which were set to be erected in appropriate places on the Shirnakh-Beyt-Shebab route, were yet to be tested for communication.

In order to set up Beyt-Shebab-Shirnakh [artillery] range service, the 1st Squadron of the 5th Cavalry Regiment was sent to Meydani-Chavush.

The Khabur Cavalry Group was in the region of Harbol-Bespin-Kita. To this group the Challek Bridge Bagoge region was determined as the new area of assembly. The Group commandership with two strong officers' reconnaissance branch would conduct reconnaissance in the direction of Keshan-Rumni, Keshan-Chamba-Bagoge. The 1st Cavalry Regiment organised an operation because of missing soldiers; 250 soldiers arrived in Gziro from Mardin on 3 September 1924. As for the cavalry battalions' missing soldiers, they were to be replaced with expert soldiers coming from the anti-aircraft battalion.

The divisional granary was in Bespin, and procurement there was made by the Army Corps. The provisions procured until then were close to one hundred tons. When the 1st Cavalry Division occupied the area of assembly, the divisional granary would have been transferred to Gewar.

Communication between the Army Corps and the Group was being carried out through mounted signal corpses. The telephone line which was built between Gziro and Jumade was being extended to Bespin. The divisional reserve ammunitions were in Gziro and were being transported in instalments to the division's region.

From time to time, the Commandership of the 7th Army Corps informed the General Staff Command about the degree of developments of preparation and the instructions he gave to the groups from his perspective:

The situation on 10 September 1924

According to the situation of the groups in the regions of operation on 10 September 1924, there was no hurdle for the Julamerk and Beyt-Shebab groups to start the operation in accordance to the instructions they received from the Army Corps. Nonetheless, for these groups to start the operation together, it would have been right to wait for the cavalry division arrive in Challek Bridge and Bagoge which were designated as the second assembly area.

When the Cavalry Division arrived in its new area, it would have passed through the Galliya-Goyan area and an opinion would have been formed as to how the English administration in the Zakho region would have faced this operation. On the same day, as a result of prior contact and communication of the commander of the 1st Cavalry Division, with the leaders of the Galliya-Goyan tribe, it was found out that this tribe would not act against our military operation, and that when the 1st Cavalry Division was assembling in the east of Hadrish-Nestorian line, due to 4-5 Nestorian villages there, this tribe would also assemble in the Hadrish-Nestorian region.

11 September 1924 Situation

According to the orders of the Army Corps, although it was decided for the Beyt-Shebab Group to start the operation on 16 September 1924, the group, upon the news that the Nestorians were fortifying since the day before, in a hill in 3355 altitude of the Nestorian high plateau, the 6th Infantry Regiment with its mountain artillery battery on 11 September at 20.00 p.m., moved to occupy the hill in 3507 altitude.

A squadron from the 5th Cavalry Regiment, a machine gun squadron and a mountain artillery battery set out in the evening of 11 September to go to Jumade. During that time, relying on the information obtained by the reconnaissance branches of the 1st Cavalry Division, that the people of Zakho region were not against our military operation, the 7th Army Commandership decided to send the Cavalry Division to other new areas of assembly, echelon by echelon, and ordered the cavalry regiment to cross River Hazil on 11 September and over Banike to march to Bagoge. On the possibility of hostile activities which may occur from the Mosul direction against the operation, the 7th Army Corps commandership took into consideration the following matters:

-to transfer, the 62nd Regiment, which has one battalion in Shirnakh, and its other battalion on its way from Mardin to Midyat, to the Khabur region;

-the 63rd Regiment which was to come to Sa´irt, to approach Shirnakh;

-the Gziro Group to be stationed in Gziro for the same reason;

-the 36th Regiment which was decided to be taken to Berwari, to be used in the Gziro region if necessary.

The situation on 12 September 1924

The flank squadron which was sent to the direction of Bir-Sivi on 12 September 1924, by the Khabur Cavalry Group, prepared its operation in accordance to the Army Corps's order. As it was approaching this village, it came under enemy fire and with the counter-fire it opened, it threw out the enemy from their trenches. Lieutenant Sinusi who attacked in order to sack the people remained in the village, came under infantry and machine gun fire and he was martyred together with two soldiers, one was wounded and five soldiers disappeared.

On the evening of the 12th of September, the Khabur Cavalry Group's divisional headquarters, the 11th Cavalry Regiment, the 14th Cavalry Regiment and mountain artillery battery were about 10 km northwest of Shiranish, its 21st Cavalry Regiment was in Shiranish, its right flank was around Bir-Sivi.

The first echelon of the 28th Regiment arrived in Van on the 12th of September. With the participation of the border battalion and the formation of a group in ´Albaq and the need to call a detachment of soldiers from the tribal division the first echelon of the 28th Regiment set out from Van to ´Albaq.

The 2nd Battalion of the 62nd Infantry Regiment which was in Shirnakh, it was ordered to leave one of its squadron in the same place and march to Jumade to be under the command of the Gziro Group.

The 36th Regiment and a mountain artillery battery, which the Army Corps decided to be taken to Berwari, were already on the march on the 12th of September.

The 7th Army Corps Commander, who was in Gziro, in order to observe closely the operation of the Cavalry Group, had left Gziro for Bespin on the 12th of September with his headquarters' forward echelon.

The situation on 13 September 1924

According to the operational order, a copy of which the 7th Army Corps Commandership presented to the General Staff Command on the 13th of September, in accordance to the instructions given earlier, the Julamerk, Beyt-Shebab and Khabur Groups were to start the operation in the morning of the 16th of September. In summary, the target and duties of the groups were:

Julamerk Group: by occupying the mountain range in the south of Beylan and establishing communication with the Beyt-Shebab Group and taking a controlling situation in the Zab Valley, it would trap the Nestorians on either side of the river, and when necessary help the Beyt-Shebab Group. The subsequent target and duties of the groups were to be given at later time.

Beyt-Shebab Group: in accordance to the previous instructions would first gain the Nestorian high plateau. By doing away with resistance which was to occur, and by being in communication with the Julamerk and cavalry groups, it would direct itself towards Upper and Lower Tiyyari region and from the Nestorian high plateau onwards would progress towards Chal by breaking the resistance also in this region.

Khabur Cavalry Group: it was to assemble in the Challek Bridge – Bagoge region on the 15th of September by sending a cavalry regiment and tribal forces to the east, on the morning of the 16th of September, set the Lower Tiyyari region and especially the Ashita village as a target, which is likely to resist in this region, and descend from the Nestorian high plateau and get in touch with Beyt-Shebab Group. The Cavalry Group, while occupying the Lower Tiyyari region with its forward and tribal forces, its large section would cover the direction from 'Amadiye and would have the occupation of the Ser 'Amadiye [mountain] range in the north of 'Amadiye as goal.

A detachment from the Gziro group which was to land to Jumade and its environs, was composed of a cavalry squadron from the 5th Cavalry Regiment, a machine gun squadron, a mountain artillery shell battery, the Cavalry Squadron of the 7th Army Corps and the 1st Battalion of the 62nd Regiment, was to form the reserve force of the 7th Army Corps, at the same time would have the duty to counteract any possible occurrences in the region and ensure the artillery range of the 1st Cavalry Regiment. Also, a cavalry squadron, a field artillery battery from the Gziro Group and the 3rd Army Corps Mountain Radiotelephone Centre was to be located in Gziro.

As the Cavalry was assembling in Challek region, it was decided that the Galliya-Goyans would assemble in the Hadrish-Nestorian region. There were four-five villages in the east of this line. The break of the resistance in this area and afterwards, together with the cavalry division, their advance to the Tiyyari region was designated them as target. Furthermore, the right flank of the Beyt-Shebab Group was to be considered for any likelihood.

The 1st Cavalry Division arranged a 200-strong force under the command of Suleymaniye Deputy Fettah Bey, gathered from a squadron of the 1st Cavalry Division Shirnakh [tribe] and Gürün [tribe], was to arrive in Urmia via Billo-Gürür route on the 15th of September and contact the Beyt-Shebab Group.

Success was desired for all in the realisation of the first target pertaining to the occupation of the region between Rivers Zab and Khabur.

When the 7th Army Corps gave this command, [the situation of] the other units which were to participate in the operation [was as follows]:

-the 63rd Infantry Regiment was in Sa'irt (on the 14th of September it sent one of its battalions to Shirnakh);

-the 62nd Regimental Headquarters and a battalion were marching to Gziro from Midyat;

-the 14th Cavalry Division Headquarters and the 3rd Cavalry Regiment were marching to Mardin;

-the 12th Division Headquarters, an infantry regiment, an artillery battalion Headquarters and a mountain artillery battery were on the march from Sarıkamış to Badlis; and,

-six airplanes arrived partly in Ras ul-'Ayn.

On the 13th of September when the 7th Army Corps commander was still 40 km east of Gziro, the operation of the Khabur Cavalry Group in Jumade according to prior instructions and separate orders was to be thus:

The 11th Cavalry Regiment with the Shirnakh tribes as forward flank would march from Bespin and over Shiranish, Banike, Balona, and Chamba arrive in the Challek Bridge – Bagoge region, the 21st Cavalry Regiment and a mountain artillery battery as a large section, would follow the forward flank, a cavalry squadron and a section of Shirnakh tribe soldiers from this regiment as the right flank over Bir-Kar, Bir-Sivi, Av-Kini, Bar-Oshki, Bar-Nona, Chiraga would go to Bagoge; a squadron from the 14th Cavalry Regiment with the detachment of Fettah Bey, which consisted of 200 soldiers from the Gürür tribe of the Goyanlis on the 12th of September would march to Harbol and would go to Rumeni over Billo and from there would be in contact with the Beyt-Shebab Group.

A cavalry squadron, a machine gun squadron, from the 5th Cavalry Regiment, under the command of the 14th Cavalry Division Brigade Commander, the 7th Army Corps Cavalry Squadron and an artillery shell battery on the night of the 13th of September would go over River Hazil to around Küsaf in Zorowa, and there a cavalry group will work to secure the [artillery] range and counteract any possible attempts to occur from the Zakho region. On 12 September 1924, the 2nd Battalion (lacking a squadron) of the 62nd Infantry Regiment, which departed from Shirnakh, was to join this group.

The General Staff Command generally found appropriate the instructions issued by the Army Corps to the group, as its [own] point of view and the order for the subsequent operation. If the English did not actively interfere during the suppression operation, as it would be necessary not to attack the *status quo* borders, especially not to cross them with regular forces, it was seen as necessary to change the instructions issued to the Khabur Group by the Army Corps concerning the operation. According to the information obtained [up to that point], as the English had border outposts in Bir-Sivi, Balona, Chaqallo and Katri, this line was not to be crossed.

Furthermore, since the Beyt-Shebab Group would occupy the Nestorian high plateau, this group would be sent either to the Upper Tiyyari mountain ridges or to the mountain ridges immediately to the north of Lower Tiyyari. In the event that the Cavalry Regiment was going to be sent to Ser 'Amadiye, it would have been on its own, it was necessary to think of the consequences for this division. For this reason it was appropriate for this division to transfer over the Develi Dağı, from Gümrü Kalesi, from the ridges of the north of the villages of Bindo, Muy, and Der-Beshki and send tribal reconnaissance branches to Ser 'Amadiye, if necessary. This way, as well as making contact with the Beyt-Shebab Group easier, the people of the Berwari region who are Muslims, would help protect the side on the cavalry regiment even if partly.

On the one hand, measures were taken to suppress the insurgence; on the other hand the situation was closely monitored. According to the intelligence reports General Staff Command received from the 7th Army Corps Commandership; although the Nestorians through various means indicated that they did not want to show resistance against the Turkish soldier, Mar-Ma´o's father Davut and an English colonel got in touch with all Nestorian leaders and gave them assurances such as "you hold out and fight for a few days. We will come to your aid. The English Government and other states will make diplomatic approaches to the Turkish Government, save you, and conclude the matter in this way", which seem to change the situation against us.

As for the situation of those tending towards the Turks, according to the information the 1st Cavalry Division Commander received about the people in the south and the tribes during the operation in the last four days, the crushing effect of the years of occupation and due to the English administration being self-seeking, the people settled in the south are more self-scarifying that those in the north and that they really want to help the government. However, due to the suppression operation being temporary and only relating to Kurdish and Nestorian events and once successful the forces would withdraw, they were taking into consideration that they would be left alone and in this eventuality they thought and feared that they would be subject to even more terrible atrocities and threats by the English. Furthermore, it has been learned that the tribes in the north were of the same opinion. Yet, if the Turkish Government extended the Nestorian operation it undertook and made serious and genuine efforts to take Mosul back, it was understood that it would be possible for all southern tribes to participate in the operation and fight against the Nestorians and the English.

The situation on 14 September 1924

The 1st Cavalry Regimental Headquarters, the 11th Cavalry Division, the 14th Cavalry Division and a mountain artillery battery in 10 km of northwest of Shiranish, 21st Cavalry Regiment in Shiranish and the cavalry group with its ring flank around Bir-Sivi, were subjected to bombardment and machine gun fire of three English airplanes which arrived from the direction of Zakho on the morning of the 14th of September at 8.00 a.m. [resulting in] three martyrs, 12 wounded, 19 wounded animals, 24 dead animals and nine animals lost. Although the English airplanes did not open fire on previous flights, the reason for doing so this time was the right wing partly crossing the Iraqi border. With this consideration, the General Staff Command warned the Army Corps, the Khabur Cavalry Group not to go over the south of the Iraqi border posts, informed the group of the situation and the flanks were taken to the north of the line.

The 54th Cavalry Regiment which was in 'Ayntab, on the 14th of September transferred to Urhoy, the second echelon of the 28th Infantry Regiment, due to be taken to 'Albaq, the regimental headquarters, the 2nd Battalion and a mountain artillery battery arrived in Van.

On the 12th of September, the 2nd Battalion (lacking one squadron) of the 62nd Infantry Regiment, which received orders to depart from Shirnakh in order to be under the command of the Gziro Group arrived in the environs of Jumade, while the 36th Regiment which departed from Badlis arrived in Sa'irt already.

The situation on 15 September 1924

Four days after the 6th Regiment and a battalion from the Beyt-Shebab Group got hold of the hill of 3507 [m] altitude on the 11th of September, a section of the Group Headquarters, the 18th Infantry Regiment and a regular artillery battalion departed to Diyari-zor on the 15th of September. In the meantime, Gawdan, Menhuran, Pavriz, Bar-Dino and Ker-Avi tribes came to the group and said they were ready to serve with 500-600 armed [men]. Their participation in the operation was thought to be feasible; furthermore it was learned that the Zel-Shirski tribe, which took refuge, was ready to serve with 300 arms.

A detachment composed of the 11th Cavalry Regiment, an artillery team and 150 tribal soldiers among the Shirnakh [tribe members] under the command of Brigadier Ethem Bey, in order to conduct reconnaissance, unite with Goyan [tribe members] and prepare a passage according to the situation, arrived in Bagoge on the night of the 15th of September, and in the meantime it was learned that the Nestorians in the Challek Bridge area escaped to the direction of 'Amadiye on the 15th of September and that 15 men, 10 women and nine children took shelter and that Chaqallo inhabited with the Nestorians. Furthermore, the 36th Regiment on the midnight of the 15th of September also departed from Omid to Mardin.

The situation on 16 September 1924

The 6th Infantry Regiment which was holding the hill at 3507 m [altitude], that day acted and cleared the range in the south of the 3355 m [altitude] hill north of Seraspido off the enemy and overtook the rear of the [riffle] range of the Nestorians in the 3355 m [altitude] hill.

Upon the Julamerk group with one section force occupying the area assigned to it (the range south of Beylan) in accordance to the Army Corps orders, the Nestorians abandoned the villages in Romashmo, Zorowa and its environs and retreated to caves in the Mount Walto. On the night of the 15th of September the detachment of Ethem Bey who came to Bagoge, entered Challek on the morning of 16 September without any incident, while the detachment of Fettah Bey arrived in Challek in the night of the 16th of September and united with the group forces. The 36th Regiment, which came to Sa'irt on the 14th of September, departed to Berwari on the 16th September.

Due to the need not to leave Badlis undefended, the General Staff Command ordered a squadron of the 63rd Regiment which came to Sa'irt, reinforced with two heavy machine guns to return to Badlis.

The operation by the Cavalry Group on 16 September was to be thus:

Under the command of Brigadier Ethem Bey, Shirnakh and Goyan tribes and the 11th Cavalry Regiment from Challek and Bagoge were passing through over River Khabur advancing to Lower Tiyyari region and started the attack in the direction of Ashita. The detachment of Fettah Bey at 3.00 a.m. passed though River Khabur and acted against the Nestorians in Bize, Alamon and Kiranosh regions. The large section of the Cavalry Group was around Bagoge and this operation was carried out with the support of artillery batteries. On the 16th of September, the 62nd Regimental Headquarters and a battalion also arrived in Gziro.

The situation of the Gziro Group on 16 September was thus:

The infantry battalion and a mountain artillery team were in Shiranish; the 7th Army Corps Cavalry Squadron and a machine gun team were in Deshti-Masek and the remaining section and the Group Headquarters were in Kita.

The report by the Prime Minister İsmet Pasha to the President Ghazi Mustafa Kemal Pasha which summarises the situation [up to that point] is at Attachment 1.

The situation on 17 September 1924

At 3.00 a.m. on the 17th September, the Beyt-Shebab Group with the support of infantry and artillery fire advanced and occupied the hill of 3355 altitude, the tribes which were with the group advanced forward with the aim of occupying the mountain ridges in the north of Ashita. At 16.00 p.m. after a short clash under the protection of the 6th Regiment, they took Ashita with no casualties. The Goyan tribes which were expected to enlist joined on the 17th of September. The 3rd Squadron of the 14th Cavalry Regiment and a section of the Goyan [tribe] on the same day advanced over Alamon and Kiranosh, and menaced the side and rear of the Nestorians on the hill of 3355 m altitude. The other [section of the] Goyan [tribe] and the Shirnakh [tribe] from the south of Alamon, Kiranosh and over Arot advanced to Ashita, followed the larger section of the Shirnakh [tribe], while the 21st Cavalry Regiment's other sections remained in Bagoge. However, because the request of the Goyan tribe for more ammunition reached the degree of insubordination, the commandership's hard reaction and warning upon which they were remorseful of what they had done, the cavalry group forced to continue its operation with one day delay and did not have any effect on the Beyt-Shebab Group taking the 3355 m altitude hill.

The 14th Cavalry Division Headquarters and the 3rd Cavalry Regiment arrived in Mardin on 17 September, [while] the 2nd Battalion of the 63rd Regiment departed for Shirnakh.

After the Julamerk Group with a section force occupied the ranges in the south of Beylan, the large section arrived in the village of Mezurqa on the 18th of September and left outposts in the ridges of the south of Beylan and in this way occupied the region up to the village of Chamba. The Nestorians who were in the location where Bubin River confluences with Zab, retreated completely to the east of Zab and hid in the caves around Mart-Maryam. The Nestorians of the Upper Tiyyari and Nestorians of Nuhub [Tuxub] gathered in the caves east and south of Mount Walto.

The Beyt-Shebab Group which occupied the 3355 m altitude hill on the 18th of September arrived to the line north of Seraspido – 4 km north of Ashita and the area of the hill of 3507 m altitude.

As the General Staff Command sensed the vital importance of the Nestorian insurgence for the country, it ordered the suppression operation administration to be carried out by the 3rd Army Inspectorate and Army Inspector Jevat Pasha to go to Omid from Erzinjan.

On this day, the second echelon of the 28th Regiment departed from Van for ´Albaq and the 36th Regiment which departed from Sa´irt on the 16th of September, arrived in Berwari. The cavalry group which was able to continue its operation, arrived in Upper Challek region on the 18th of September, the Nestorians in the villages of Alamon, Bize and Kiranosh retreated to Ashita.

The attack of the estimated 600 Nestorians against the Beyt-Shebab Group on the front of the 6th Regiment was crushed with a counter attack, and as a result most of the insurgents were killed and some of them, together with the Nestorians nearby, retreated to Berwari in a wretched state.

The situation on 19 September 1924

According to the plan the 7th Army Corps Commandership presented to and approved by the General Staff Command regarding the operation from then on, after the Nestorian high plateau was conquered with the help of the cavalry group and the Beyt-Shebab Group, Ashita was to be occupied and the Beyt-Shebab Group was to advance to Chal. In the meantime, appropriate arrangements were to be in place for the cavalry group in the west of Ashita region, an infantry regiment from the Beyt-Shebab Group was to be assigned for reconnaissance for the area between the River Zab and Khabur, the Beyt-Shebab Group Headquarters and its other regiment to transfer to the east of Zab. This way the first stage of the operation up to Zab was to be concluded and the second stage of the operation between Julamerk, Gewar, and Shemdinan was to be conducted. For the time being, if there were no extraordinary difficulties, it was considered not to take the cavalry group any further to the east, as the distance extended food supply difficulties were increasing.

The 62nd Regiment was be assigned for the work to secure the area between Khabur and River Hazil.

The 14th Cavalry Division Commander Suphi Bey was ordered to come to Gziro with his headquarters, and when he arrived the 5th Cavalry Regiment and a field artillery and artillery shell batteries were to be assigned under his command, and this force to be assigned the duty to secure the western region of River Hazil. The field further east of River Hazil was not suitable for the movement of field artillery and artillery shells batteries.

As for the operation of the cavalry group in the Ashita region:

On the 19th of September the clash that started in the north-western hills of Arot, because of the reinforcement of our forward forces could not continue for long time and the enemy retreated. The group forces which were advancing in the direction of Arot, because of the hurdles in the field, took control of the mountain pass in about two hours east of Arot only after the sunset and took measures to spend the night and a squadron from the 14th Cavalry Regiment and a section force separated from the tribes held the ridges south of Arot.

The 14th Cavalry Regiment, the 21st Cavalry Regiment (lacking two squadrons) a battalion and the Gürür [tribe] under the command of Hüseyin Agha, were again subjected to enemy fire in the ridges to the southwest of Ashita and after counter fire and quite a short skirmish and the retreat of the enemy again, advanced up to Ashita, and the 14th Cavalry Regiment, the 21st Cavalry regiment and the 11th Cavalry Regiment spent the night respectively in Ashita, in the hill of southwest of Ashita and around Ashita.

The situation on 20 September 1924

At 14.30 p.m. three English airplanes attacked the 2nd Battalion of the 62nd Regiment, which was going from Bespin to Shiranish, for three hours and dropped about 500 bombs. In this air raid, the commander of the 8th Squadron First Lieutenant Sadullah and six soldiers were martyred, 25 soldiers (15 heavily, 10 lightly) and nine animals were wounded.

The 11th Cavalry Regiment which spent the night around Arot and the tribes located there departed at 9.00 a.m. and came to Ashita and united with the Beyt-Shebab Group Headquarters.

In the order that the General Staff Command gave to the 7th Army Corps, to stop the English air raids rapidly, requested [the Army Corps] to spread rumours as propaganda in Zakho and 'Amadiye regions that if there was another English air raid in the north of English outposts in Bir-Sivi, Balona and Chaqallo, it would be understood that the English insist upon not recognising the *status quo* borders, [so] the army would be free in its operation and retaliate and for the inconveniences to befall in the retaliation the English would be directly responsible.

On the 17th of September, the 12th Battalion of the 63rd Regiment which departed from Sa'irt reached Shirnakh on this day and a squadron from the 3rd Cavalry Regiment, which arrived in Mardin, was sent to Nsibin.

The situation on 21 September 1924

The large section of the Julamerk Group, which on the 18th of September occupied the region up to Chamba village, on the 21st of September from Mezruqa crossed over River Zab and together with the detachment that occupied Zorowa, advanced to Mount Walto. Both forces occupied the villages of Sırta, Mart-Maryam, and Hedyana and besieged the caves where Nestorians were located and ask them to surrender. They were also informed that if they did not surrender artillery fire would open on the caves. The English reconnaissance and raids were continuing without intervals. This day at 15.30 a.m. the English airplanes coming from Zakho opened fire with machine guns our convoy of camels in the south of Shiranish around the village of Deshti-Masek; forty camels were killed, 20 camels and two camel drivers were wounded.

Facing this situation which in many respects made the operation harder, the 7th Army Corps proposed to the General Staff Command: "As we do not have defensive arms against the airplanes, the only [artillery] range suitable for the movement of supply branches necessarily passes through Shiranish and as the continuous attacks of the English airplanes in 15-20 km distance to our [artillery] range, it is no longer possible to transport on this line and food supplies problems have appeared. Our convoys which were assigned the duty with difficulties - basically with payment of rent and persuasion - disperse and escape when there are air raids.

In order not to leave our operation - which is about to conclude - in difficult circumstances, in terms of food supplies and transportation, and to secure our [artillery] range, which goes from Gziro to the east, it is necessary to stop the English air raids, through diplomatic means or extend the operation from Zakho to ´Amadiye."

The Chief of General Staff was not of the same view. According to him even if Zakho was occupied, the English airplanes could still fly and since their speed was 180 km per hour they could stay on air for three hours and continue bombarding Julamerk, Shirnakh and Gziro Regions for about an hour without any problems. For this reason, since they insist on attacking our transportation of range, we need to restrict every type of operation carried out on the Shiranish-Bagoge line to the night, to have soldiers and animals during the day safe from air raids and try to down the attacking airplanes with machine guns, to reduce casualties.

In the meantime, because of the first air raids the diplomatic efforts on the English were continuing even more effectively. If despite this the airplane raids continued, it was strongly possible to decide to occupy Zakho and ´Amadiye. But the possibility of this occupation being ineffective and forcing the English to conduct air raids even to a greater degree was also a strong probability. Therefore, since staying in the occupied places could not affect the outcome, we could sustain more casualties. For this reason it was necessary to go wherever the English airplane fields and facilities were, destroy them and stop the English raids. With this consideration it was necessary to start immediately the operation, with these possibilities with new preparations and once ordered use forces sufficient to achieve the objective and continue the operation until the end.

On this matter, the General Staff Command, as well as asking the opinion of the 7th Army Corps Command and the 3rd Army Inspectorate, proposed the same viewpoint to the Office of the Prime Minister. In this proposal it was pointed out that due to our shooting range being close to the English air fields, if with great sacrifice it was taken to further north, with the snow to fall in a month at most, circulation would be prevented, we would be forced to evacuate the places which were entered at the expense of the blood of our soldiers and in the end the Nestorians would return to their old places. In this eventuality the tribes of the region would be opposing the government and with the increase of the effect of the propaganda they would have a tendency towards the English; and at a situation would emerge, whereby our government would have lost politically and not achieve its objective. The English who knew this situation very well without seeing the need to attack our operating forces, continued the air raids in a tiring manner on the shooting range which passes near the *status quo* borders, with obstinacy and insistence peculiar to themselves and in four days caused casualties of 14 martyrs (one of them an officer), 43 wounded (15 of them heavily). Against this, if we restrict ourselves to diplomatic efforts and not actively reciprocate the airplane raids which would continue on our forces, it would especially destroy the morale of the tribes as well causing many casualties.

If one looked at the continuation of the English air raids on our shooting range within the *status quo* borders despite the diplomatic efforts, and according to the intelligence report our Urmia Consul presented to our Foreign Affairs Ministry, [the English] taking volunteer soldiers from Suleymaniye and its environs and transferring them to the Rewanduz region, it was clear that whatever decision the League of Nation was going to make to resolve the Mosul question, the English decided to resolve it with arms. In order to dissuade the English from their intentions and objectives and prevent in an effective way their airplane raids, we needed to explain clearly that we would not insist upon not crossing over the *status quo* borders; that in the same manner we also decided to resolve the Mosul question with the force of arms and protest to the English with a 24-hour notice, and forcefully that despite our initial protestations the air raids continued on our forces in the north of this line and caused heavy casualties. If they did not end [their raids] and the English insisted on attacking, the responsibility of the situation would have being entirely theirs and our side would not have to abide and our army would have been free in its operation and if despite this strong protestation the air raid continued in any of our regions, our forces needed to immediately occupy Zakho and ʾAmadiye.

The General Staff Command was in the opinion that on the face of such a strong effort the English would decide not to attack. Because the English were in an unsuitable position in Egypt, Sudan, Iraq and Hedjaz [the General Staff Command] did not think that [England] would risk a war with Turkey for the resolution of the Mosul question. At the same time, bearing in mind the possibility of the English stubbornness and persistence in attacking, the [General Staff Command] proposed the necessity to take into consideration the occupation of Zakho and ʾAmadiye not being sufficient that until the English were completely thrown out Mosul the operation to be widened and for this the necessary mobilisation to be done and take requisite measures.

The General Staff Command which considered the possibility of a war with the English at the end of the Hakkâri operation, in order for the 7th and 5th Divisions and 1st and 14th Cavalry, 2nd and 17th Infantry Divisions, 28th, 36th [Infantry regiments] and the 34th Infantry Regiment, which was being prepared to be sent for the 9th Army Corps, to be ready for mobilisation, asked the National Defence Ministry to procure arms, ammunition, clothes, material *etc*, necessary for the mobilisation and to dispatch them henceforth.

The 2nd Squadron of the 63rd Regiment reinforced with two machine guns, ordered on the 16th of September to depart from Sa′irt, departed on the 19th of September and arrived in Badlis on the 21st and the 2nd echelon of the 28th Regiment which departed from Van on the 18th arrived in ′Albaq on this day.

The situation on 22 September 1924

Since the regular and tribal forces of the Julamerk Group besieged the caves where the Nestorians were located and warned them to surrender and under the support of machine gun fire advanced up to the Mount Walto, around Nuhub [Tuxub] River, up to the section of the Sendar ridges there was no Nestorian presence left. Due to Nestorians' insistence on not surrendering, on the same day artillery fire opened to the caves around Mart-Maryam and hit the mark inside some caves. Even though the bandits were asked again to surrender, the insurgents insisted on not surrendering. On the night of the 23rd of September, three-four Nestorians who came out of the caves and went down to the river to collect water were killed after fire opened [on them]. On the day of the 24th of September in the section over the Mount Walto in the hills to the north of Nuhub [Tuxub] River, there were no Nestorians left. As it was learned from later reports, the Nestorians who resisted against the group were about 40 and other than those who got stuck in the caves, together with Malik İsmail, except for Malik Khoshaba, all Lower Tiyyaris escaped to ′Amadiye. The people they left behind in the caves were five women, one of them wounded, one ill, and eight children. First aid was give to the wounded and a section detachment and tribal forces were set to follow the escapees, though no one was caught.

According to the report the Army Corps commander presented to the General Staff Command, due to difficulties faced up to then in the procurement of food supplies it has not been possible to take advantage of the operation conducted by the Julamerk Group.

The 14th Cavalry Regiment which was in Bindo on the 27th of September retreated in echelons against an attack by the Nestorians who came from 'Amadiye with an estimated force of 500 and equipped with machine guns. The Nestorians plundered the village of Bindo and burned it down so the villagers retreated to Ashita.

The General Staff Command anxious about completing the operation as soon as possible, ordered the occupation of Mount Walto by the Julamerk Group and stated that the area of operation concerning the Nestorian question could not be counted as occupied and ordered the necessity to occupy Chal actively and of our advance patrol stations to be sent to the south, up to banks of Zab.

On the question of the 7th Army Corps Commandership' concerning the measures to be taken after the operation, according to the view put forward by the General Staff Command, as the League of Nation had learned of our views and the English views on the Mosul question as a result of the investigation, it decided that the matter ought to be negotiated a little while later. When the English took this matter to the League of Nation, they were under the impression that they were preparing a milieu of a strong disturbance in Turkey. So much so that, they were under the impression that they ensured the introduction of sedition and disturbance to the forces used for suppression of such an uprising.

The successful suppression of the Nestorians and the speedy elimination of the provocations for internal uprising prevented the English to be successful during the negotiations in the League of Nations and to assume an attitude of being in control of the situation. For this reason, the English wanted to prolong as far as possible future negotiations and revisit provocations for sedition and disturbance - which they planned early but could not realise - to control the political situation. The decision of the Turkish Government was for Mosul to come into its possession no matter what. It was possible that the League of Nations would have investigated *in situ* before the second round of negotiations. Because of this possibility and the need to inform the world public opinion that Mosul did not want to stay in English hands, [it was necessary] not to allow the English to eliminate by pressure and force of the [then] current public disorder in the Mosul province and work for the continuation of the people's discontent with the English and the uprising, and assist in any way we could our compatriots in Mosul in this matter. In this manner, during the possible League of Nation Investigation Committee investigation and during the new round of negotiations, it was necessary to prove this fact and resolve the matter in our favour. Nonetheless, since it was not possible to do this without regular forces it was imperative to do it with a special organisation.

In order to ensure Sheikh Mahmut's resistance in the Suleymaniye region, the Suleymaniye Group ought to be helped by any means and manner.

Since Simko was being sent to the Rewanduz Region, the Rewanduz Group needed to be reactivated again and help the Suleymaniye Group in a secure way.

With a special organisation to be arranged by the Army Corps, local organisations needed to be set up in Zakho, 'Amadiye, Shigur [Sinjar] and Mosul regions and this organisation to be continuously reinforced and extended.

It was necessary to establish communication with the El-'Abid tribes who inhabited in the western and southern regions of Mosul and were are always against the English administration and in uprising [at that point] and benefit from 'Uceymi Pasha, the organisation of the resistance of these tribes needed to be reinforced and extended. Thanks to this organisation, the public disorder that emerged in Mosul as a result of the English occupation by force, it would have been extended to the point and strength that the English would not have been able to suppress, even if they used force. In order to prevent the continuation of situation, the English would have taken[111] forceful measures and in the meantime they would [no longer] conduct air raids on our forces in the north of the *status quo* borders and further to the north. Such a situation would be protested immediately and if occurred again, in order to prevent air raids, the English airplanes headquarters would be destroyed in a series of raids. Nonetheless, as at that point there was no need to take those absolute measures, the detachments were not going to attack the borders if the General Staff did not order them [to do so].

During this period, it was seen appropriate for the forces to take these positions:

-Once the targets of the Nestorian operation have been met, the area between Chal and River Khabur needed to be covered with a border battalion;

-The forces to be stationed in Gziro, Sa'irt and Mardin regions;

-The 1st Cavalry Division and the 2nd Infantry Division assigned to the suppression operation to be given time to rest.

-The other detachments to support the organisation in Mosul and control the situation in the borders.

-If necessary, this force to be reinforced with other detachments and this organisation to be actively protected and attacks that may befall on our country be prevented. With this aim the forces to be taken to these places:

---

111. There seem to be a typographical error in this passage. The Rapporteur says "the English would *not* have taken [*yapmamaları*] . . ."; however, the context indicates the opposite: "*yapmaları*".

The 1st Cavalry Division:	To Mardin and its environs;
The 2nd Infantry Division:	To Sa´irt, Gharzan and Midyat region;
The 17th Division; composed of	To the region south and west of River Hazil
The 62nd, 63rd and 36th Regiments:	(Especially due to the importance of the Shiranish region to be held and its fortification);
The 14th Cavalry Division:	Its headquarters and 5th Cavalry Regiment to be left in Gziro and the Cavalry Regiment in Mardin to transfer to Nsibin;
The 28th Regiment:	To stay in ´Albaq.

The 2nd Infantry Division for the time being to be under the command of a brigadier and Nurettin Pasha to transfer to the 17th Division.

All forces should be secured and warned that the English could conduct an air raid at any time.

In order to reach the region of Chal and occupy the area in the south up to Zab, if the 2nd Division forces were deemed sufficient, to send the 1st Cavalry Division to the Mardin Region henceforth.

Although the 3rd Army Inspector Jevat Pasha was in the same view with General Staff Command, concerning the measures to be taken at the end of the suppression operation, he was in the opinion that the activity of setting up a special organisation beyond the borders to be ill-advised. As for the Commander of the 7th Army Corps Ja´fer Tayyar Pasha, he pointed out that after the suppression operation reached its goal, if the retaking of Mosul was shelved, the tribes could again turn against us, that it would not be possible to maintain public opinion in our favour until the second round of negotiations in the League of Nations, that the English have taken measures to control the situation and that they may conduct air raids on our forces to the north of *status quo* borders, so much so that to accept the possibility that they may send the Nestorians from the direction of Zakho and ´Amadiye and attempt a military operation, that in this eventuality, rather than benefit from the tribes, to the contrary may suffer harm, and that he was in the opinion that by means of a manoeuvre and propaganda to rid of the Nestorians and station a strong force in Gziro against Zakho and ´Amadiye, and that the success to be achieved in the Mosul question could be cancelled by stopping the operation in this manner. Concerning his thoughts on the arrangements the forces should take, he stated that [the area] between Chal and Khabur could not be covered with one battalion, and that even if it were possible to compose this battalion with local tribes, they could not be trusted and with this consideration at least a regiment was needed. Yet, even for this, due to food supply difficulties, it could not be possible either, that to be strong against ʾAmadiye could only be possible by occupying the Berwari Region, including Ser ʾAmadiye and benefit from the food supplies in that area and in order to ensure this situation, [points out] the need to send new forces to that region.

Due to the completion of the operation, tribal forces were dispersed, while the Nestorians gathered in ʾAmadiye with Nestorian forces the English reinforced from the south and were being reorganised. Likewise, due to food supply difficulties, in the area the 1st Regiment was stationed, it was not possible to post forces that were needed to be stationed in the south of Oramar and Shemsdinan and around Zab. To extend this success which was achieved at great expenses and sacrifices and control the situation until the liberation of Mosul, it was only possible with the occupation of Zakho and ʾAmadiye. Even though the political situation was not suitable for the occupation of those places, if this occupation was decided because of Mosul it was necessary to reinforce the Army Corps.

Due to the retreat of the insurgent Nestorians to the south after conceding captives, around the time of completion of the suppression operation (28 September 1924), General Staff Command, sent a communiqué to the 7th Army Corps Commandership and the 3rd Army Inspectorate, to thank first the army corps and army commanders, as well as all group commanders, officers and soldiers for achieving success despite all hurdles in the field with real life-sacrificing efforts and asked this [message] to be disseminated to all the commanders and soldiers, and at the same time wished that the success that was achieved to be extended to the first target set for the occupation of the region of Chal.

The 7th Army Corps Commandership issued orders to the units concerning the measures to be taken after the operation, informed the General Staff on 29 of September 1924 and asked for the operation to be postponed until orders were received.

The General Staff Command, as a response to the 30 September dated report by the 7th Army Corps, on the 2nd of October instructed that:

-Since no one is left in the east of Zab, the suppression operation was actually concluded.

-It was possible to occupy Chal with a section of the Julamerk Border Battalion and local tribal soldiers;

Since the delegates of the parties in the League of Nations decided the *status quo* borders to be protected by our side, come what may, there was no need for our forces to stay where they are, and since food supply was not possible to take new measures according to prior orders.

-Taking into consideration the possibility of the Nestorian and Iraqi forces in Shiranish with the support of the English airplanes, and in contravention of the agreement in the League of Nations, attacking just like the attack which occurred in Bindo, to take the measures so ordered, not to allow to be subject to similar attacks in isolated situations and especially to fortify Shiranish quickly and forcefully and set up quickly a secure line of communication between Shiranish and Gziro.

-The border battalion which needs to be set up between Zab and Khabur, as it would rely on outposts to be set up in this region and it will form a buffer against the south, to be composed of tribal soldiers.

-It was necessary to discharge *en mass* the soldiers who completed their military services, after the new measures are taken, and inform the office of the Prime Minister, National Defence, Foreign Affairs and Internal Affairs about this situation.

In another order of the General Staff Command on the same day (2 October 1924):

Although the occupation of Rewanduz until the 21st of September was desired, as sufficient money could not be sent to Simko's detachment, winter was approaching and the Nestorian operation was completed, it was too late to benefit from sending Simko to Rewanduz.

In the future, if decision is taken for a joint operation, in order to make efforts for an operation in the Rewanduz region, not to allow Simko to move away and to release the soldiers of the border battalion which were given his command.

The 3rd Army Inspector, who was charged with the responsibility of the operation administration, arrived in Omid on the 2nd of October and informed the General Staff Command that as of the 3rd of October he was going to take *de facto* command.

According to the 3rd Army Inspector's orders, the new arrangements for the forces were to be as follows:

-the 1st Cavalry Headquarters and two cavalry regiments to Mardin and its environs;

-one regiment from the 1st Cavalry Division to Omid;

-the 14th Cavalry Division Headquarters and a cavalry regiment to Gziro;

-one cavalry regiment to Nsibin;

-the other cavalry regiment to Urhoy;

-the 2nd Cavalry Division Headquarters and its 18th Regiment to Sa'irt;

-the 6th Regiment to Midyat;

-the 1st Regiment to Gharzan Region;

-the artillery regiment of the division to Eruh;

-the 17th Cavalry Division Headquarters and two infantry regiments to the region of both sides of River Hazil;

-the 36th Regiment to Shirnakh, with the proviso that it will be under the command on the 17th Division;

-from the artillerymen in this group, one mountain artillery shell battery assigned under the command of the Division and a field artillery battery were taken to Omid;

-one battalion from the 28th Regiment stayed in Van, the remaining sections went to 'Albaq.

As for the information the 3rd Army Inspectorate provided about the enemy:

-All Nestorians escaped towards the direction of 'Amadiye and that they were around 5,000 and that they took shelter in a steep mountain around 'Amadiye.

-Although information was sent that Malik Khoshaba was in the west of Zab, it was also explained that since all Nestorian villages were evacuated, it was strongly probable that Malik Khoshaba escaped to the south.

-Due to the completion of the operation, new arrangements were being made for the detachments, while in Ankara diplomatic contacts were continuing.

Upon receiving a diplomatic note the General Staff Command in an order issued to the 3rd Army Inspectorate [instructed]:

According to the diplomatic note issued by the English on that day, they requested that the forces stationed at the point starting in the confluence of River Hazil and Khabur, through the line that passes through the east of River Hazil and north of Mount Neri-Nar and immediate south of Neri, which is the centre for Beyt-Shebab, Julamerk and Shemsdinan, to retreat by noon, 11 October 1924, and informed that if they did not, from that day on they would be free in their operation to secure this objective and order their forces in Iraq accordingly.

The *status quo* was decided with the acquiescence of both sides unanimously, in the League of Nations on the 30th of September. For this assertion which was clearly contrary to the situation [at the time], our government informed both the British Government and the League of Nations, that the English violated the League of Nations latest decision, and that [the Turkish Government] refuses the allegation and assertion in the diplomatic note, and that it protested it.

At the same time, it was accepted that the English would in reality attack our units with their air and infantry forces, from noon 11 October, and in accordance to the instructions issued beforehand it was necessary to take measures and apply these measures until that day.

Not to resist between Zab and Khabur;

Especially the region of Shiranish, to the west of River Hazil, to be gained no matter what, and that for this reason the region be fortified and reinforced rapidly and fend off forcefully all kinds of attacks that may occur in this region; to enable our forces which departed to go to the west of Zab and Khabur regions to make new arrangements, to arrive in the areas assigned to them, which is only possible by holding onto the Shiranish region.

Not to allow the various echelons of the forces which are on the move to be attacked separately by the English;

In order not to sustain many casualties, generally from air raid and shake the morale of the forces, the matter of the operation being conducted at night, was specified.

According to the information the 3rd Army Inspectorate gave to the General Staff Command, on 11 October 1924 the forces were to be:

-the 21st Regiment of the 1st Cavalry Division in Gziro;

-the 14th Regiment of the 1st Cavalry Division in Bespin;

-the other section of the Division on the march to Bespin;

-the 7th Army Corps Cavalry Squadron in Gziro;

-the 2nd Battalion of the 63rd Regiment in Harbul;

-the other battalion of the 63rd Regiment on the march to Shirnakh;

-the 36th Regiment in Shirnakh;

-the 1st Battalion of the 62nd Regiment in Shiranish;

-the 2nd Battalion of the 62nd Regiment in Banike and its environs;

-the Beyt-Shebab Group forces in Elki;

-the Julamerk and ʹAlbaq groups in the same place.

A force composed of 200 infantry soldiers, eight machine guns, ten packed horses and a major from the Beyt-Shebab group and four squadron commanders was left in Ashita. Furthermore, it was stated that the 62nd Regiment, against the possibility of attack by the English on the caves, could make use of hollow rocks as shields and in places where it was needed added same types of shields and they were in a position to face an attack.

The General Staff Command did not see the situation as secure as it was thought to be and described and gave an order to the 3rd Army Inspectorate to be more cautious and alert.

As it is accepted that the 62nd Regiment, which is to stay in the east of River Hazil, does not have sufficient number of soldiers, even after the new arrangements, which were decided to be made, this force could not successfully counteract possible English ground and air attacks, it is appropriate to send reconnaissance patrols in indeterminate times of the day to the region of Shiranish, east of River Hazil and maintain mobile outposts in the region.

Although, we have the upper hand and the right in the political circumstances, it is necessary not to allow the English to gain an easy military success and exaggerate such a success to strengthen their propaganda.

If it is likely for the large part of the Cavalry Division to be in the east of River Hazil in the evening of the 11th of October and the 62nd Regiment in the region, this division together with the 62nd Regiment, on the day of the 11th of October, to get out of their positions and march through the west of River Hazil. This march which will cause the English to attack our units from air, even on the ground, without waiting for the deadline date, would not be successful, as the time is not suitable for this march to be done in the morning of the 10th of October. The cavalry regiments together with the 62nd regiment, under single command, to counteract possible English attacks in the afternoon of the 11th of October, and gain time until the evening of the 11th of October to march, with the proviso of absolutely not leaving this march to the day of the 12th of October, to transfer to the west of River Hazil.

If the large section of the Cavalry Division went westwards of the 62nd Regiment's region, and if only the cavalry forces could be taken to the west of River Hazil as of that night, the 62nd Regiment should not be left on its own in known English shooting ranges; the need to transfer take to the west of River Hazil after taking measures against airplane reconnaissance and attacks, was specified.

The change the General Staff Command made to the original concentration plan on the Nestorian Operation was as follows:

In the original plan, the 3rd and 16th Divisions would have concentrated in the Omid region. As two regiments from the 12th Divisions were assigned to the command of the 7th Army Corps in the operation for a possible mobilisation, [General Staff Command] changed its mind about sending the 3rd Division. Likewise, because the 16th Division was sent to Manisa, [the General Staff Command] decided to send the 17th Division in its stead due to its proximity and leave the 1st Cavalry Division in the region it was stationed. The General Staff which saw this change as necessary and was waiting for the conclusion of the investigation by the League of Nations, though both sides accepted to maintain the status quo of the 30th of September, if an English attack occurred, as well as protesting at the League of Nations, we would declare that would be free in our operation and the modified plan will be put into practice in parts. To this end, for further mobilisation of the forces still under the 7th Army Corps command, and the 5th and 7th Divisions Ministry of National Defence was asked to send the requisite arms, ammunition and other equipment and address the need for officers by preference in the event that a plan for concentration was put into practice. The 3rd Army Inspector was asked of his opinion on the forces being stationed in the concentration region, regiment by regiment.

Moreover, on the 11th of October, the Chief of General Staff, Fevzi Pasha, in a report he presented to Ghazi Mustafa Kemal Pasha informed that our forces between Khabur and Zab were marching in the direction of Sa'irt over Beyt-Shebab in order to winter and that they completely vacated this area. The 1st Cavalry Division was on the march towards Mardin to winter, two regiments were still between Chamba and Shiranish and that together with the 62nd Regiment they received an order to defend themselves against an attack by the enemy and that this force leaving mobile outposts between River Khabur and River Hazil, was to march to Bespin and Gziro.

In the event of an English attack on the disputed *status quo* border between Zab and Hazıl, the light covering forces would retreat to the west of River Hazil by degrees and with mobile detachments they are going to send from time to time would ensure this region's state of belonging to us.

The English airplanes everyday bombarded our forces and cause casualties and it is corroborated that the enemy has significant forces in the northwest of 'Amadiye, in the south of Bindo.

Although the suppression operation ended, the General Staff Command considered the seriousness and significance of the position, on 12 October requested from the Ministry of National Defence [the following]:

It was decided for the National Assembly to discuss the situation which emerged as a result of the latest diplomatic note by the English. In the meeting of the night of the 11th of October, the Ministerial Council decided to postpone the discharges of soldiers entitled to be discharged and call [to arms] the second group of the 1902/03-born soldiers, while waiting for the assembly's decision.

In accordance to the Ministerial Council decision, the 2nd Division battalions under the 7th Army Corps command to be increased to 600, and the other forces to increase to maximum capacity needed for the Peace Corps.

Officers and soldiers on leave to join their units immediately.

Except for the extant soldiers of 2nd Division and those on leave rejoining their units, it was understood that the other requests could not be fulfilled due to legal difficulties. Consequently, the General Staff Command in the written response to the Ministry of National Defence explained again the seriousness and importance of the matter (Appendix 2).

The General Staff Command saw the possibility of being given the duty to assemble the forces again in the Gziro Region to prevent English attacks, in accordance to the decision to be taken by the Assembly, and informed the 3rd Army Inspectorate in order to wait for the 2-3 weeks within which the decision is thought to be taken, to postpone the transfer of the forces to their new regions and while waiting for the decision, the 2nd, 17th Infantry and the 1st Cavalry Divisions to be generally stationed within the districts of Shirnakh and Gziro and asked which forces should be suitable for which regions.

Upon this decision, the arrangements the Army Inspectorate made were as follows:

-The 14th Cavalry Division Headquarters, the 3rd Cavalry Regiment and the 7th Army Corps Squadron in Nsibin;

-The 5th Cavalry Regiment in Eruh;

-The 1st Cavalry Division around Gziro;

-The 17th Division in the west of River Hazil in Bespin and its environs

-The 36th Regiment in Shirnakh;

-The Beyt-Shebab Group in Elki;

-The Julamerk Group in Julamerk;

-The 'Albaq Group in 'Albaq;

Although the General Staff command saw these arrangements as appropriate, in the event that the Julamerk and Beyt-Shebab groups, which were composed of the 2nd Division forces, stayed in Julamerk and Elki, whatever the decision of the National Assembly, the field situation in the operation that needed to be conducted and especially because of the season, it would not have been effective. Likewise, due to communication difficulties coordination of action was not possible, and because of food supply difficulties, these forces were not to be taken henceforth to within Shirnakh and Gziro districts. Furthermore, due to the news received about signs of uprising around Van and Badlis, and in the event that such a situation could not be suppressed, it would have grown, it would have been necessary to take into consideration the use of more forces, [so] the machine gun squadron of the 5th Cavalry Regiment of the 14th Cavalry Division which was still in Gziro, reinforced with two artilleries from the Divisional mountain artillery battery, were to be sent immediately to Badlis under the command of the 2nd Division Commander and Badlis Governor Kâzım Pasha.

[The General Staff Command] also ordered the squadron from the 5th Cavalry Regiment which was assigned the duty to protect the range between Shirnakh and Meydani-Chavush, to join its regiment.

At the end of the diplomatic activities, which continued in Ankara by means of exchanging diplomatic mores, there was agreement that the matters should be resolved through the League of Nations. In the meantime, because of the Grand National Assembly decision on 19 October 1924, the General Staff Command ordered the 3rd Army Inspectorate that the provisional arrangements were no longer necessary and as informed earlier to take the forces in the regions to where they were to winter.

After the conclusion of the operation, the situation which maintained its seriousness for a while was resolved in this way, the General Staff Command in the circular sent to the 1st - 9th Army Corpses, except for the 1st and 2nd Army Inspectorates and the 7th Army Corps, since the Hakkâri Operation was completed, it specified the stations of the army corps and division headquarters which participated in the operation.

According to the circular:

-the 7th Army Corps Headquarters in Omid;

-the 2nd Division Headquarters in Sa'irt;

-the 17th Division Headquarters in Gziro;

-the 1st Cavalry Division Headquarters in Mardin; and,

-the 14th Cavalry Division Headquarters in Nsibin.

The General Staff Command accepted the fluidity of the political situation of the time and saw it appropriate for the 3rd Army Inspector to stay in Omid until the Mosul question was definitely resolved.

In the end, the provisional border line the League of Nation decided in the meeting held in Brussels was communicated to the parties and consequently the parties accepted at the border region to be left to civilian administration and the military units to be stationed at the rear of this line.

The situation of the parties was as follows on in the beginning of November 1924:

The situation of the 7th Army Corps

-The 7th Army Corps Headquarters in Omid

-The 2nd Division Headquarters in Sa'irt

-The 18th Regiment in Sa'irt

-The 6th Regiment in Midyat

-The 1st Regiment in Gharzan

-The 2nd Artillery Regiment Headquarters, Heavy Mountain Artillery Battalion in Sa'irt

-A Krupp mountain artillery battery in Eruh

-17th Division Headquarters in Gziro

-The 62nd Regiment in the east and west of River Hazil

-The 63rd Regiment in the east and west of River Hazil

-The 2nd Division mountain artillery shells battery on Kendi-Hadid

-A heavy radiotelephone station in Gziro

-The 1st Cavalry Division Headquarters, two cavalry regiments and a mountain artillery battery in Mardin

-A cavalry regiment in Gziro

-The 14th Cavalry Division Headquarters and the 3rd Cavalry Regiment in Nsibin

-The 5th Cavalry Regiment and two mountain artilleries in Badlis

-The 54th Cavalry Regiment and two mountain artillery shells in Urhoy

-The 28th Infantry Regimental Headquarters, one battalion of the 28th Regiment and No. 4 Mountain Radiotelephone Centre in Van

-The other battalion of the 28th Regiment in 'Albaq

-Number 2 and 3 Radiotelephone Centres in Mardin

-The 7ᵗʰ Army Corps Cavalry Squadron and a field artillery battery in Omid.

-The situation of the English, Indian and the Nestorian forces:

-An Iraqi cavalry regiment in Sinjar, Tel-'Afar and Pesh-Khabur

-An Iraqi infantry battalion, two mountain artilleries in Zakho

-A Nestorian battalion in 'Amadiye

-A Nestorian battalion in Aqra and Zibar region

-Two Nestorian battalions, 400-500 under Sıdda; two English mountain artilleries in Rewanduz

-A Nestorian battalion, in Koysanjak

-A Nestorian battalion an Indian battalion, A Levy cavalry regiment and four mountain artilleries in Arbil

-A Nestorian battalion, an Iraqi infantry battalion, a Levy cavalry battalion, two English infantry battalions, four English mountain artilleries, four English *obus* (12-round), 16 armoured vehicles, 40 airplanes in Mosul

-An Indian cavalry regiment, an Indian armoured vehicle squadron in Kal'et-ul Sherefat

-An Iraqi infantry battalion, armoured vehicle squadron (four vehicles) in Chamchamal

-A Levi cavalry battalion, an Iraqi cavalry regiment and a Nestorian battalion in Suleymaniye

-An Indian infantry squadron, an armoured vehicle squadron in Kafri

-An English infantry battalion, an Indian cavalry regiment, An English cavalry regiment, 12 English mountain artilleries, eight English obus (12-round), an Iraqi infantry battalion, an Iraqi mountain artillery battery, two Iraqi armoured vehicles, four Iraqi airplanes, 45 English airplanes in Baghdad

-One Iraqi cavalry regiment in Nasiriye.

An Iraqi cavalry regiment from Suleymaniye and a Nestorian battalion went to Rewanduz and the remainder of the Sıdda forces in Rewanduz were taken to 'Amadiye.

It was expected that the English would amass forces in the Zakho region from locations nearby. Nonetheless, no information had been obtained as to the size of this force.

According to the information received from our London Embassy, the English divided their armoured vehicles to four squadrons composed of 16 armoured vehicles, that is a total of 64, and by dividing their airplanes into nine squadrons in all, they increased them to 150 and they had a radiotelegraph team of 200 extant soldiers.

Ebubekir of Zibar, from Rewanduz's tribal leaders, informed the Sapatan Border Squadron on 6 October that the English made Kâni-Watman, 20 km west of Rewanduz, as their centre, send their soldiers to 'Amadiye and Zakho and had their soldiers in Rewanduz crossing over Zab to Dizan.

Conclusion

The suppression operation conducted under difficult condition of those days, against the Nestorian uprising, which started with English incitement and support by them using force, did not reach an absolute conclusion concerning the insurgents, and most of the insurgents escaped to outside of the borders. Essentially, this matter, which the English initiated at the end of many difficult political and military battles was accepted as resolved by the parties retreating to either side of the [border] line and both accepting to be partly in their favour. In reality, the Turkish forces could not achieve success to affect a decisive resolution, neither on the insurgents nor on the Mosul question.

APPENDIX 1

PRIME MINISTER İSMET PASHA'S REPORT TO PRESIDENT GHAZI MUSTAFA KEMAL PASHA SUMMARISING THE STATE OF AFFAIRS UNTIL THE BEGINNING OF THE OPERATION

Ankara, 16 September 1924

To his Excellency Ghazi Mustafa Kemal Pasha

Response to the communiqué of 21 October 1924 of the Army Office

1. Our forces will start the suppression operation today (16 September 1924).

2. The Julamerk Group (one infantry regiment, one heavy artillery battery) will come to 15 km southwest of Julamerk in the Beylan High Plateau and control Zab.

The Beyt-Shebab group, composed of an infantry regiment and a heavy mountain artillery battery, is at the hill in 3507 m altitude, 20 km south of Beyt-Shebab, and an infantry regiment and a mountain artillery battery at the northeast of Elki, under Nurettin Pasha's command, will march to the Nestorian high plateau and control Lower and Upper Tiyyari regions.

The 1st Cavalry Division assembled in the Challek-Bagoge region, about 25 km south of Beyt-Shebab and over River Khabur, with a section will march to the Lower Tiyyari region, while its larger section will cover and spy on the direction of 'Amadiye and facilitate the advancement of Beyt-Shebab Group.

3. The first target of these forces is to control the Nestorian region between Rivers Khabur and Zab. After that, it will march to the east of Zab and toward Chal.

4. A force composed of a squadron of cavalrymen and tribal soldiers, separated as the right flank during the move from the 1st Cavalry Division assembly point in the west of River Hazil to the assembly point over

River Khabur. When this force approached Bir-Sivi on 12 September 1924, it was subjected to gun fire from the English border patrols there; our forces repulsed the outpost soldiers. Our contact with the English consisted of this [incident]. Perhaps for this reason the English airplanes attacked our cavalry forces which did not cross the *status quo* borders. Furthermore, 3-4 days before the arrival of our forces, the Banona centred Guli [Galliya-Goyan] tribe leader Sadık Agha who is serving in our army, took the arms of the soldiers of the English outposts in Banona and drove them away. Nothing new arrived after this incident.

5. During the assemblage of our forces around Julamerk, Beyt-Shebab and Khabur, former parliamentary deputy Yusuf Ziya who was in Badlis, received a telegram on the 31st of August, from his brother Lieutenant Rıza, the *aid-de-camp* of the 18th Regiment from the Beyt-Shebab Group. [On this telegram] he said: "I am waiting for your response to prepare the draft on the amount so ordered". Yusuf Ziya's response was: "I am going to Erzurum. There is no need to determine the amount. Send money immediately and quickly. Inform Bahattin and Faik, with no regard to my arrival. Bahattin is Ziya's brother and he is a civil servant in Erzurum. Faik is his brother-in-law. He is in Badlis.

Yusuf Ziya on 11 September sent Faik the following telegram from Erzurum: "My departure to Ankara is dependent on Rıza sending money. Let me know of the information obtained from him."

On 12 September Faik gave the following response to Ziya: A week ago, through Hajji Mehmet, Rıza got a draft for 300 lira; I cannot understand why you have not received it. I sent the sheep to Sa'irt. If they are sold I will send you [the money?]

After Yusuf Ziya was arrested he sent Faik the following telegram: I have been arrested, I would not be able to go to Ankara. I have no longer need for the money. Investigate where it is.

Later, Yusuf Ziya when he was in the village of Wartanis, in the Mosul Plain, mentioned that the Beyt-Shebab Group would abscond on the sixth day of September.[112]

6. Four officers and about 400 soldiers from the 18th Regiment which were part of the Beyt-Shebab Group and where Ziya's brother Rıza was the aid-de-camp, on the night of the sixth of September absconded. Telegraph communication and Yusuf Ziya's mention of the desertion before the incident, caused us to assess that including the desertion of the forces, he organised an uprising in Van, Badlis and Sa'irt regions and that during this uprising he wanted to hide that he was in Erzurum or that he personally arranged it or that he wanted to ensure support and

---

112. Yusuf Ziya Bey was court martialled as the instigator of the desertion of the Turkish soldiers during the Nestorian operation. He was sentenced to death and executed; Anzerlioğlu, *op.cit.*, p. 146.

participation in Erzurum for this purpose. It is deemed likely that the general arrangement were made by the English, as one of the absconding officers joined the English in Zakho. All the people mentioned have been arrested.

7. The Kurdish tribes' leaders in the regions where the cavalry division passed said they were very happy that the Turkish forces and the Turkish Government were returning and that they were ready to join with their retinues.

8. The careful observation of the Straits' *sub aqua* has been ordered.

9. The general apprehension that could be observed is in a normal and expected state. As we have not sensed anything out of the ordinary and especially thinking of the financial and commercial situation we did not want to show much flurry and with this thought we did not want to inform the pres about the events. We are considering all the aspects of your trip so that it progresses calmly and normally. In any case, until you arrive in İnebolu the situation is bound to be clearer.

APPENDIX 2

THE GENERAL STAFF COMMAND REPORT DEMON-STRATING THE EARNESTNESS AND THE IMPORTANCE OF THE SITUATION IN THE NESTORIAN OPERATION

Ankara, 23 October 1924

To the Ministry of National Defence
Response to the communiqué of 21 October 1924 from the Army Office

1. The Mosul question does not as yet show a clear and visible form. The English on the one hand are gaining time by creating various situations and preparing for diplomatic negations, and on the other they consider the matter of being stronger in Iraq as very important. The declaration of martial law in the northern section of the Mosul province, the officers on leave being sent to their units in Iraq, the transfer of the centre of the forces in Iraq to Mosul, the English being active within Iran as well, the Minister for the Colonies personally going to Mosul by airplanes and conducting inspections, at the same time asking the Prime Minister of Iraq on behalf of the Iraqi Government to go around for visits in all the sanjaks of Mosul and conduct inspections, and according to the latest intelligence, a powerful English fleet departing for Basra, indicates that the English consider the Mosul question quite important.

2. If the situation today continues to be unclear, just like the political situation preceding the Balkan War, the General Staff Command which is responsible for preparing the country's means of defence and maintain its forces, cannot see as appropriate the discharging of any class of soldiers who are serving or the postponement of calling [to arms] of any class of soldiers who need to serve under the law and need training immediately.

3. If the government which is cognizant and in control of the political state of affairs, renders the general situation to be calm and free from

danger and approves the discharge of soldiers who are legally to be discharged and not calling [to arms] of the second group of 1902/03-born, then I submit the General Staff will act in accordance to the decision of the government

Signature
Fevzi

PART C

DOCUMENT 2

DOCUMENT FROM THE SWEDISH ARCHIVES CONCERNING THE GENERAL STAFF OPERATION AGAINST ASSYRIANS IN HAKKÂRI IN 1924

(Original text in Swedish and French)

Legation of Sweden
Presenting official Turkish explanation of recent events in the Mosul border

Constantinople, 11 October 1924
No: 178 1 Enclosure
NP 51.

158 B.25.8.24.

London 21/10

His Excellency
Mr Baron E. Marks von Wärtemberg
Minister for Foreign Affairs

Mr Baron

The English protest note to Turkey concerning alleged Turkish violations of the status [quo] at the Mosul borders is fresh in memory.

It was said in passing to the Turkish Foreign Affairs Ministry's current delegation here first on the 30th of September - the same day, as newspapers here could publish its text after the telegram from Geneva - and thus was not yet known, in Angora [Ankara], when Lord Parmour submitted it to the League of Nations.

When one recalls the adventure of the Governor of Hakkari in August, one hardly needs to look for the explanation in the English note concerning the events.

It was indeed natural that after the insult, for which the Turkish Government has been exposed through its most senior representative local person, a [general] staff expedition against the guilty "Assyrian" tribes ought to follow, and it was probably also reasonably clear that this could not take place without the fear spreading to other demarcations lines, where they threatened the leaders to pull back with their people and that as a consequence, the perception could arise there perhaps subject to the good faith of the English border commander, that the Turks stood in theory to carry out an invasion of Mosul District.

Perhaps also different opinions about the exact route of the demarcation line played a role - although it certainly must seem like a weak point in the English account, which was particularly emphasized, that at the "local military unit", which really would have had conflicts with the Turks, should not be accompanied by some British officers.

To illustrate the opposite side's understanding, I have the honour hereby to submit, in the corrected French translation, one of the official newspaper in Angora Hakimiyet-i-Milliye ("Rule of nation"), which on the 9th of this [month] published an account of the relevant reasons of the [general] staff expedition and the course of events, which as reported to me by Nusret Bey, was developed by the Turkish General Staff. (The report relied on the deputy of Amadiye in the Baghdad, Parliament, *Haji* Reshit Bey, who apparently belongs to the majority, who at the vote in June on the Anglo-Iraqi Treaty either stayed away or voted against it.)

The official Turkish response to both of the above-mentioned English notes and another recent one, which was submitted on 5th of this [month] and requested that the Turkish troops retired to some distance from the demarcation line, was said to have been taken in possession yesterday and probably today or tomorrow will be forwarded to the British representative here.

Johannes Kolmodin

Translation[113]
Hakimiyet-i Milliye
9.10.1924

The Nestorians who had been armed and equipped by the English, just after the armistice, to replace the released British soldiers, returned with their weapons and their ammunitions to the interior of the Province of Hakkari, on the eve of negotiations for Mosul, which did not fail to worry our tribes and destroy their tranquility. In a note presented to the Parliament of Iraq, Naji Rashid Bey of Berwari, deputy of Amadiye, protested against the illegal delivery of a quantity of weapon and ammunitions to the Nestorians of the vicinity of Julamerk, during the release of the English military service, which had the result of encouraging them to attack persistently the Muslim tribes of Berwari and its vicinity. This protestation demonstrates the reality of fact, and the well-grounded of complaints formulated by our tribes on the side of the Government of the Republic.

While the Nestorians armed by the English civil servants of Iraq – as the aforesaid document of the deputy of Amadiye proves – were being sent to the interior of Hakkari, the English civil servants themselves came in and had a meeting with the governor of Chal Evliya Bey. At that moment alarming rumors circulated about an attack by the Nestorians from the south with Persian cooperation, and our tribes reiterated their requests of assistance from the government. These alerts and these movements which emerged the day before the conference of the Golden Horn, could not however distract the Government from the purpose, which was proposed not to influence the started talks; also it did a duty to appease and reassure the tribes and to bring no change in the military situation of these regions.

It was at that moment that the Vali Halil Rifat Bey who went for inspection from Julamerk to Chal, with an escort of gendarmerie, in the zone occupied by Nestorians, in the vicinity of Hangedik, fell in an ambush on 7 August 1924. Under fire from the Nestorians the commander of the escort and four gendarmes were martyred and the governor and five gendarmes were wounded. It goes without saying that it was necessary to pursue and to deliver to justice the leaders who encouraged by the south had even the audacity to attempt to commit an assassination of the Governor of Hakkari. Also the government of the province, prevailing over the right that the general status of the provinces confers on them, seen the insufficiency of the numbers of the gendarmerie, decided to send a detachment of soldiers to the place.

---

113. The newspaper article was submitted to the Minister in French.

While concentration of force of suppression was made in the region of Beyt-Shebab, they had the chance to come across of a new proof of British connivance. Four officers, Ihsan, Tevfik, Rasim and Hourshid [Hurşit], on the pretext that the operations began, left the headquarters with the men who were under their orders. But the following day, the aforementioned, realizing that they had been deceived and sensing the treason of their officers, turned back and retook their camp. One of the treasonous officers, Hourshid [Hurşit], faithful to the instructions which he had accepted previously, went to Tahub [Tuxub, Txuma] to join the British agents.

On the 16th of September our troops concentrated in Gezira, Beyt-Shebab and Julamerk. Before initiating the operation, the command displayed a notice outlining the purpose of the government and declaring that the armed forces had as mission to foil the activities of the Nestorian bandits of Tahub [Txuma] and to bring the agitators to justice. The people and tribes complaint to authorities had therefore nothing fear and could go about their affairs in complete peace under the protection and diligence of the Government. After which the troops united and marched in the direction of Tahub [Txuma] there.

The moment where our conscripts of Gezira crossed Hezil Su [River], on the north of the demarcation line fixed in 1918 by the English field marshal, advanced to complete their mission, always inside our borders, they were exposed to fire of the British planes. An officer, several soldiers and many animals were killed. Contrary to truth, the English Authorities of Iraq claimed in London that the air attack had been aimed to counter the irregular Turkish [forces] crossing Hezil Su and because these had violated the established status [quo] and the concentration had caused intense emotions among the population of Zakho at Amadiye. Now, the reality was that the English planes opened fire against the regular troops, which far from violating the status quo, neither crossed the demarcation line established by the British nor reached the first English post. The only aim of the British aerial attacks was evidently to prevent the operations of our forces which was carrying out against the Nestorians advancing parallel to the line of demarcation to the inside of our borders.

Respectful of the orders received, our forces entered the region where the insurgent Nestorians were located, despite the air attacks of the English, which resulted with the death of a certain number of innocent people and the destruction of several villages. Arrived at their destination, they launched a second announcement declaring once again that the culprits will be pursued and surrendered to the rigor of the law. They then proceeded to pacify the region by heading only against those that had raised the black flag and opposed to their advance, with weapon in hand. The persons who were compliant were not worried at all. So was accomplished, fast and peacefully, the mission of our troops, charged with restoring order and tranquility in the land.

Julamerk is the capital of the province of Hakkari. Hangedik is located on the highway, which then leads to the south south-westerly direction along the upper river Zab over Chal (the last major town north of the demarcation line) to Amadiye. Zakho lies west of Amadiye towards the Tigris, as well as the English side. Tahub [Txuma] would be somewhere in the mountainous east of the Upper Zab (south of Julamerk but still in the Turkish zone), where overview maps also include a couple of Chaldean names, which suggests a Nestorian district.

DOCUMENT 3

DOCUMENT FROM THE SWEDISH ARCHIVES REGARDING DEPORTATION AND MASSACRES OF ASSYRIANS IN 1925
(Original text in French)

UD:s 1920 Års Dossie
HP Vol. 1481, 5-6, 1925
Mosul-frågan

LEAGUE OF NATION

Communiqué to the Council　　　　　　　　C.799.1925.VII
11/47909/25888　　　　　　　　　　　　Genève, 11 December 1925

BORDER BETWEEN TURKEY AND IRAQ

The notes of a Chaldean Catholic priest, transmitted by the Union Catholique d'Etudes Internationales (Catholic Association of International Studies)

The following report which is among the list of messages received from the non-official international organizations, by Abbot Paul Bedar, a Chaldean priest from Zakho, is forwarded to the Council for information on the request of the British delegation.

REPORT OF THE RECENT DEPORTATION
OF ASSYRO-CHALDEAN CHRISTIANS FROM ZAKHO BY
THE TURKS

These are Christians (about twenty villages) of the Goyan region in the district of Zakho. This region is precisely in the zone disputed by the Turks and the English and is located on the current Turkish-Iraqi border. Since last year, the Ottoman troops intended to invade Iraqi camps in the vicinity.

In September 1925 these troops were suddenly put in action, cutting of the Christian villages, surrounding them and removing dozens of residents to Anatolia. Some European newspapers reported the events sceptically; the Turks denied the incident formally with a misleading impudence, but the well-informed English press reproduced the incident with precision. We waited for confirmation or denial of the news by domestic sources, and two letters arrived from Zakho, entirely confirming the disaster and recounting it in all its brutality. Here are the principal sections of these two letters. It is a relative and friend of mine who wrote to me. In the first letter, dated by September 26, 1925, he says:

"Dear abbot

Being in Paris, I do not know if you heard of the disaster that struck our Christian population of the mountains. The facts are: in June this year the Turkish commander of the Goyani forces arrested the Chaldean priest of the village of Marga, Father Benyamin, and sent him to Gezira [Jazire] in irons. During the trip, his clothes were torn to pieces and his beard was ripped off. From Gezira, they sent him towards Mardin. We were told that he died of starvation. The Turks gave him nothing to eat and he was reduced to beg to passers-by to get some breadcrumbs. During the last hour, we have been told that the unfortunate abbot Benyamin was dragged in this manner up to Amid [Diyarbekir], where he was thrown into a horrible dungeon. I would not know whether he is still alive or dead.

The Turkish commander told the Christians here, that the case of the deported priest was political, and that they themselves had nothing to fear. Finally, with promises and their protestations of loyalty, the Turks managed to lull the poor Christians.

Suddenly, a few days ago, the Kemalist troops spread in the area, surrounded our Christian mountain villages and deported *en mass* until the last inhabitant. The turmoil was at its peak, children's and women's rose into the sky. Most were taken away in their night clothes. A number of children fell dead of fear to the ground and were crushed. The others were pushed back and forth – there was total confusion. It was heartbreaking to hear babies cry, calling their parents in the dark. In the end the villages were rummaged through and entirely depopulated.

It goes without saying that the Turks together with the people also carried with them all their possessions: cattle, belongings, foodstuffs, etc., leaving the habitat completely looted. They dragged over 8,000 Christians. But, as you know better than me, the area is very mountainous and completely wooded, and many of these deportees escaped from the enemy and run away to us in Zakho, Iraqi village. The others made their escape in the second or the third day, but reached us in a state of destitution and fatigue - some of them were almost naked, others had not eaten in two or three days. As I write this, almost a quarter of our Chaldean deportees fled during the deportation and arrived in Zakho.

The survivors say that prisoners' condition is heartbreaking. I will write to you continuously as other refugees will arrive. Father, pray for these poor victims. News of the deportees and the sight of the survivors break our hearts. Nothing sadder than this."

A few days later I received, the second letter, dated 21st of October, which complemented the first. My relative says that:

"Everything I wrote in my first letter about the deportation of our Assyro-Chaldeans from Goyan Mountains is completely and literally true. My report was very brief; here are now further details, both on those who managed to escape and of the deplorable situation of those who remain in Turkish hands. The refugees having been able to save only their skin now live scattered around Zakho, destitute, dying from hunger and cold, without shelter, without clothes, without supplies, because of the high costs, not to mention the famine here. I have to tell you that our harvest in the plain, this current year is almost entirely absent because of locusts, so that for our other people in the plain nothing can be done to help these poor folk. The English and Iraqi governments have provided for the most exigent necessities. But what can the government alone do for these thousands of victims, who lack everything? Our government itself is in great discomfort this year because the harvest has failed throughout the Mosul area, the granary of the State. Grasshoppers have devoured everything, and government revenues have been next to nothing. Everything has already become very expensive and we have the greatest concerns. These thousands of refugees are therefore doomed to perish of hunger and misery. They seem to be almost 4,000 - more than half of the deportees managed to escape from their guards and get to Iraqi territory.

As for those who are still in the hands of the invaders, mostly women and children, their situation is simply awful, according to those who escaped. One of them says: when all the people from our villages were gathered and mixed together, the Turkish command entrusted us to an escort composed, I believe with the worst people in earth. In any case, I cannot possibly imagine that there may be people who are more ferocious, more inhuman, more brutal than these guards. They forced us to walk the entire day, even the old people of 70 years of age, as well as five year old children. I cannot think of the kids, their memory give me pain in the stomach. To see them walk for ten hours in these steep mountains, pushed, jostled, thrown or dragged across the ground by these barbarians! I simply turned my eyes away, because I could not endure this gruesome sight. But what to do with my ears? I could not avoid having to hear the children crying. Their cry, their sob, their twitter and wail - tears me soul, I swear! And throughout this terrible walk without either food or drink, we were whipped by the Turks.

On the first day we stopped in the evening. Our guards crammed us, drawing a circle around us in the open air and called the Muslim inhabitants of the village in front of which we stopped. They invited them to a human fair. When the Muslim [Kurdish] villagers assembled, our guards lined us up, exhibiting us, displaying us plainly as merchandise in front of buyers. Finally, the children were sold for one *mejidiye* each (five franks). Some were sold for clothes, others for a basket of grapes or for a chicken. The human market contained unspeakable scenes. They sold a child and they left the mother to be deported the following day, and the poor mum plunged to the ground, sprawling in the dust and pulling her hair asking for her child, whom they took away, running after him calling his name; and the child convulsed in pain and bursting in tears in the claws of the barbarians. The maniacs soon overcome both of them: using sticks and riffles silenced the child and forced back the mother. On the other side, in a scene no less cruel, the husband was brutally separated from his wife; she was sold to a Kurd from the village, and the husband was detained to be deported. God saved me from the sight of further horrors. The same night I succeeded slipping past the guards and managed to flee, but what I saw during those twenty-four hours was enough to turn my hair white a few weeks."

Another prisoner, who escaped on the fifth day of the deportation, comes to complete the narrative of the atrocities committed by the Turks against the poor folk who were deported:

"We walked for five days. But I cannot comprehend how we walked, how we managed these five mortal stages. I could not tell you. All I know is that one third of the people died so that the roads were covered with their bodies. That's because we walked on empty stomachs. The Turks gave us absolutely nothing to eat. In the evening, after the end of the day's march we stayed at a Muslim [Kurdish] village, where the guards displayed us to buyers and stuffed themselves with the money they received for children and young women, let the rest of us, for a quarter of an hour, to go and beg for some bread. But most often the fanatical villagers pushed us away with abhorrence or even showered us with insults and with blows. In a period of a quarter of an hour they reassembled us to spend the night in the open air in a region where icy wind was blowing. None of us could close our eyes.

All you heard was the poor prisoners moaning and groaning over the hardship of the day and the chill of the night. The following day at dawn we were put on the march. In actual fact, most of our men were crawling or dragging themselves up rather than walking and they could not take it anymore. Surprised by the removal, half of the deportees were bareheaded and barefoot, and then buzzed under the breath of the fresh icy wind while the feet resembled grindstones, so much were they swollen having to jump on the pebbles of the road - and always on an empty stomach. Our guards would sometimes give food to some young women who then subjected to despicable acts which I cannot talk about. Thirst tormented us as much as hunger. Our bowels were dried out by hardship, fatigue and anxiety, our thirst was indescribable. The Turks never let us extinguish our thirst. These barbarians even just as we approached us a stream or a water source, suddenly forced us to take another road and drove off us in a direction not expected to find any water.

Driven by hunger and thirst we hung on to the trees along the road to detach a few leaves and we devoured them in the guise of food and drink. At other times, we raided wild plants and herbs off the fields to appease our hunger, which had made us, what one might say, mad. In fact, some of us had lost our minds and rambled on, on the account of all that we suffered. Along the way we dragged people who were more dead than alive but pity those who lingered and remained behind! The guards mercilessly beat them to death. They therefore died walking or rather during the march. For the rest, for my part, I do not think that any of our people whom I saw at the last instance, could survive this fatigue and to see their paternal home again."

So are the stories of the escapees, my dear abbot, which are similar and at the same time complement each other. For these tested people I can only beg you to pray a lot, and make their misfortune and their critical situation known in Europe, if you can. Farewell and be well!

It is striking, that the story of the deported Assyro-Chaldeans in September 1925 is entirely consistent with what of the Armenians who were deported in [1916].[114] When I consult the notes I made concerning this massive deportation of Armenians, where I collected testimony from the deportees, I find the same atrocities, the same violations.

I could have added to my notes other abominations, other details to the painful reports of the Assyro-Chaldean refugees themselves, but on reflection, I have decided to confine myself to their own, rather succinct statements, in the knowledge that the victims' own voice is surely more eloquent than anything I could say. Only one thing remains to point out: none of them who have gone through six or seven daily marches will survive their hardship as our last narrator affirms and will ever return to their home country.

This is precisely the aim of the Turks, to eliminate the Christians by means of deportations, which make less noise than big massacres. They pretend to put a stop to imagined Christian intrigues; in fact the Turks by moving people from one place to another they intend to terminate, to exterminate them - and they succeed only too well! The old Ottoman

---

114. The correspondent made a typographical error stating 1926 as the year of deportation.

did not know this refinement of cunning cruelty. Here, there is a cure seemingly sanctimonious, but terribly effective.

Over 1,000,000 Armenians were deported during the Great War, or their skulls are still strewn over the ground in the plains of Mesopotamia. They all perished. I remember, by the way, that an Armenian deported from Erzurum, told me when he arrived in Zakho, in 1916: "Father, we left Erzurum as 16,000 captives - see for yourself what remains of us."

When the Armenian caravans from Erzurum marched across the bridge of Zakho, they enumerated them officially: of the 16,000 deportees there remained only 400 wretched individuals, almost all dying. The following day they were forced to march towards Mosul. I was present. Some twenty of them threw themselves over me, begging me to keep them, not let them leave, while they screamed that they were sure to die on the road. But who could at that time to defend or protect the Armenians? It was a crime of high treason (*lèse d'Etat*). So were the Armenians crushed.

Now that the Armenians no longer exist, the Turks attack the last representatives of the Christian faith in our neck of the woods, the Assyro-Chaldeans. Already in the summer of 1924, in the same month of September, more than 20,000 Assyro-Chaldeans of the Tiyyari District were suddenly assaulted by a major force of Turkish troops; and not being able to fight back abandoned their homes and fled towards Mosul, and a great number of them perished of deprivations in the caves, during the last winter. One thing is for sure, the Assyro-Chaldeans are entirely at the mercy of the Young Turks. Unless the European states to put finally an end to these horrible atrocities, the Kemalist depravities, I say, the Western powers abandoning the last remnants of the glorious Assyrian people and leaving them at the mercy of the wild Turanians, the world will soon be able to see that not one of them remained any longer, and the Christianity that flourished in this renown region nearly for two thousand years, entirely disappeared under the blows of the elated Turks!

By Abbot Paul Bedar
Chaldean priest of Zakho.
Paris, 20 November 1925

COLLECTION OF DOCUMENTS 4

DOCUMENTS FROM THE SWEDISH ARCHIVES REGARDING DEPORTATION AND MASSACRES OF ASSYRIANS IN 1925

(Original text in Swedish)

Telegraphic Agency [Kungliga Telegrafverket]
D. No 219/281, Br. HP, AFD. 33, Mål 13

Document 4a

Telegram 10 December 1925

In the Council meeting of September it was decided to post the Estonian General Laidener [Laidoner] to Mosul to the investigation of border troubles, pending the Council's final decision on the border between Iraq and Turkey. The up to date published reports point out that incidents which took place in the border during the summer and autumn has been insignificant and unavoidable as long as the border question has not have been settled. Furthermore, it is pointed that about 3,000 Christian refugees arrived from the Turkish area and that this number increases every day.

From the hearings held with the refugees is clear that those displaced by the Turks after shocking atrocities and arrived in Iraq are in an extremely distressed state. The reason for these deportations, it is impossible to comment on without hearing the Turkish explanation and without an investigation of the north of the Brussels line, which has not been possible because of the Turkish opposition to extending then General's mission to survey the north of the Brussels' line.

Boheman

Document 4b

Telegram, 16 December 1925

Additional report from General Laidener [Laidoner] now published on deportation of Christians from the area north of the Brussels' line.

Through that it is noted that on 1 November the number of refugees was 2,800, but that this number now must be over 3,000 when every day new refugees arrive in Iraq. The refugees are in a completely destitute state. According to the general and his members' testimony included show that Turkish troops under the direction of officers entered the villages north of the Brussels line in March almost immediately after the Commission's departure, and subsequently often returned.

Initially, the soldiers had merely asked for money but later claimed livestock, grain, and the inhabitants' women. Women have been particularly vulnerable and often their husbands, when they arrived together, have been massacred. The same fate met those who in any way opposed to the Turkish soldiers' brutality. The report includes detailed documentation of the Turkish soldiers committed violations.

Boheman

Document 4c

Telegram, 16 December 1925

In the report presented to the Council in the afternoon it was suggested that the Council, based on the findings of the Mosul Investigation Commission, it shall decide that the border between Turkey and Iraq are determined in accordance to the demarcation line established in Brussels in October 1924.

The British Government was requested to submit to the Council a new treaty with Iraq through the placement of the current mandate of the government for to a period of 25 years.

As soon as, or within six months from today's date, found by the Council that this condition has been duly fulfilled, the Council's decisions concerning the border line becomes definitive.

Further, it is requested that the British government, as a mandate power under the auspices of the Council take administrative measures to ensure the Kurds local autonomy, and as faithfully as possible to follow the Commission's recommendations on amnesty, protection of minorities and commercial measures.

The report first gives the issue a historical treatment before the Council, with particular emphasis on mediation attempts. Furthermore, it is noted in the study the Investigation Commission discussed two special solutions, namely to allocate Iraq the area throughout the south of the Brussels line or extension of the area which follows a line, essentially the little Zab, but that the investigation commission members after receiving the other Council members' opinions, with the exception of the parties, discontinued that solution, as most likely to fulfil the task, assigning the Council under Article 3 of the Lausanne treaty.

It also notes the importance attached by the Commission to the preservation of the mandate and points out to the Council it could not make Brussels Line definitive until full certainty achieved and that this condition fulfilled.

Boheman

DOCUMENT 5

TELEGRAM BY JOHAN LAIDONER CONCERNING TURCO-IRAQI BORDER DISPUTATIONS AND DEPORTATION OF CHRISTIANS

(Original text in French)

17 November 1925
Mosul

After investigation on the spot I have the honour to give you to the following information on the situation. Firstly, Turks carried out deportations of Christians [who have] currently taken refuge in the Zakho region and every day news arrive. According to testimonies given by the refugees, they obliged them to leave their villages by force and violence. The Turks committed atrocities [and] massacres on the Christian population. It is impossible to define the true cause of deportations without explanations from the Turkish side. However we could note formally that all Christians were forced to leave their dwellings because those arriving in Iraq are without means of support, having to leave all their belongings in the villages.

Secondly, Turkish authorities had taken to the practice of sending military posts and patrols to the village of Nuzur. Having visited different border areas, I could note with a certainty based on description of this line that Nuzur is in the south of the Brussels line. The maps are not correct. The British authorities have told me their intention to install a station in Nuzur. I have advised to leave all the stations on current location until the [League of Nations] council session [is held]. Allow me to advise you to invite the Turks if possible neither to install a military station nor to send patrols to the south of the Brussels line during the same period. After personal reconnaissance on the spot, I could affirm that villages Sinat, Der-Shish, Nuzur, Sul, Rusi, Hurki and Arush visited from time to time by Turkish patrols, are located in the south of the Brussels line. Also it could be noted note that currently there are no Turkish posts in the south of Brussels line.

Thirdly, Turkish protests about British over flights of the northern area of the Brussels line could perhaps owe to the fact that the Turks considers that the [Brussels] line passes through the southern villages named above, which are indeed regularly flied over by British planes.

Fourthly, before border question is definitively settled, my opinion is that incidents pointed out under numbers two and three are inevitable and cannot consequently influence in an unfavourable way, whatever the decision of the council. On the other hand deportations Christians could continue, which deserves council attention.

COLLECTION OF DOCUMENTS 6

ARTICLES FROM TIME MAGAZINE

Document 6a
Monday, Dec. 28, 1925, at Geneva

Backed by Occidental public opinion, the Council of the League of Nations handed down two unanimous decisions of the first importance last week:

MOSUL. The vexed question of whether the Republic of Turkey or the British-protected Kingdom of Irak shall hold sway over the oil fields and Christians in the Vilayet of Mosul (TIME, Dec. 31 et ante) was illuminated early in the week by the report of the Esthonian General Laidoner, sent by the League to investigate British charges against the Turks (TIME, Oct. 12).

Turkish Atrocities of the perennially familiar type were reported by Laidoner, whose lack of sentimentality or easily shocked squeamishness is ably attested by the fact that he once ordered 130 Esthonian Communists shot in a batch because they were about to start a revolution.

General Laidoner began by recalling that the Turks had refused his commission access to the region on the Turkish side of the Mosul frontier. He then went on to say that the commissioners had cross-examined refugees from this region before there was any possibility of their having been tampered with by British agents. In conclusion he expressed absolute certainty as to the material fact that the Turks have been deporting the non-Moslem inhabitants of this region with frightful barbarity.

Specific Charges: 1) In September the village of Merga was surrounded by 500 Turkish soldiers under Colonel Backy [Baki]. After separating the women from the men and children, the entire population was deported in two columns. Two men and three girls were shot without reason; five old women were buried alive under large stones because they were unable to keep up with the march.

2) At the village of Alto four men and seven women were killed, and all the comely women outraged during a forced march under Turkish guards to Be-Gawda.

3) During their deportation from Billo to Geznakh, a ten days' march, the women of Billo were separated each night from their husbands and families and violated by Turkish soldiers and officers, who did not hesitate to kill those who resisted.

4) The 62nd Regiment of Turkish infantry was responsible for these and innumerable other acts of violence and pillage.

General Laidoner concluded, in speaking of the witness-refugees:

> "These Christians are Chaldeans who have lived in this region for centuries as serfs of Kurdish chiefs, who last spring refused to carry out orders from Angora to massacre them. . . . They are a home-loving people, never rebelled, and were the backbone of Kurdish wealth. . . . All idea of voluntary emigration on their part must be excluded. The mere fact that they arrived at Irak and are still arriving daily in the utmost physical distress and completely without resources proves beyond doubt or dispute that they were compelled to abandon their villages by force and violence. . . .
>
> "They showed no hesitation in replying to our questions and we never found any contradiction among the statements made by persons from the same village. . . . The Turks rounded up and deported these people on the pretext that war was about to break out between Irak and Turkey."

The Turkish Position

Foreign Minister Tewfik Bey sent an official protest to the Council, alleging that England had armed the Chaldeans against the Turks and that no Turkish atrocities had been committed. Unofficially the Turks at Geneva inquired, "How much did Laidoner get paid for his report?" Previously the Turkish representative before the Council, Munir Bey, had delivered an interminable harangue in which he raked up endless legal quibbles. He alleged that the Council had no right to dispose of Mosul, under the Treaty of Lausanne, except by a unanimous decision in which Turkey's vote must be counted.

When Signer Scialoja, Acting President of the Council, informed Munir Bey that "unanimous" was to be understood as "unanimous except for the votes of either Britain or Turkey, the interested parties," the Turks walked out, declaring that they had no authority from Angora to accept such a vote. This action amounted to flouting the League of Nations and the World Court, the latter having ruled that under the Treaty of Lausanne the Council was competent to adjudicate the dispute (TIME, Nov. 30).

The Council's Decision. Before Signer Scialoja handed down the Council's ruling, he went through the form of asking the ostentatiously absent Turkish representative to appear and be seated. After a pause of 15 minutes, the Turks sent in a message that it was impossible for them to attend the meeting. The Council then ruled as follows:

1) The present Mosul frontier to be moved in such a way as to give Turkey a very small increase of territory.

2) The Vilayet and Village of Mosul to be definitely acknowledged as part of the Kingdom of Irak.

3) Britain to renew her treaty obligation to protect Irak for an" other 25 years, unless within that time Irak is admitted as a member of the League.

4) Britain to conclude a commercial treaty between Irak and Turkey, allowing Turkey to use the trans-Irak trade routes.

The Significance

Well informed observers opined that, while there is a bare chance of war, Turkey will in all probability be given sufficient commercial inducements to keep her quiet.

Document 6b

Monday, Oct. 12, 1925, Mosul

Attempts to settle the question as to whether Turkey or Great Britain shall dominate Mosul (TIME, Oct. 5 et ante) were featured last week by a modicum of practical action and the continuance of heated bluffing at Angora and London.

Action was confined to two definite announcements. The Permanent Court of International Justice at The Hague set Oct. 22 as the date to decide (at the request of the Assembly of the League of Nations) whether the League Council has authority to adjudicate the Mosul matter. Meanwhile the Council of the League despatched General Laidoner, onetime Commander-in-Chief of the Esthonian Army, at the head of a League commission to investigate British charges that the Turks have been deporting Christians over the Mosul frontier.

Bluffing on the part of the Angora Government began by calling four more classes to the Turkish colors, the massing of four divisions of cavalry at Gezira, 20 miles behind the Mosul frontier, and mild efforts to prepare the Dardanelles against a possible naval threat from Britain. The Jumhuriyet, famed Turkish Government journal, announced: "They are merely measures of national defence . . . since the emasculate League of Nations wallows as a mere servile instrument of British dictatorship. A recourse to arms remains as our only means of defending our rights."

From London it was announced that "merely by coincidence" a strong British fleet will soon be manoeuvring in Near Eastern waters. L. C. M. S. Amery, Secretary of State for the Colonies, who precipitated the break with the Turks at Geneva (TIME, Sept. 28), almost paraphrased Turkish utterances: "I can imagine no action more fatal to the honor of Britain than for us to abandon our rights in Mosul."

From the Archbishop of Canterbury, Primate, went a strongly worded letter to Premier Baldwin asserting that "there would be a widespread sense of shame among Englishmen if the Government were to abandon Christians in a British protectorate to the Turks."

COLLECTION OF DOCUMENTS 7

The Gertrude Bell Archive: The Letters[115]

Document 7a

[24 September 1924]
Baghdad, Sep. 24

....

We're in the uncomfortable position of not knowing whether we are at war or not. There are some 3000 Turkish regulars inside our administration frontiers busy killing our Assyrians who are flocking down as refugees once more. There are about 7000 of them up in those mountains but one imagines that a considerable number of them have been killed. We don't know. Meantime H.M.G. says nothing and negotiations on the frontier question continue to go on peacefully at Geneva. That's the position. Isn't it remarkable?

---

115. Source: The Gertrude Bell Project < http://www.gerty.ncl.ac.uk/> [accessed on 14 January 2009].

Document 7b

[21 January 1925]
Baghdad, Jan. 21

....

I had Roddolo to lunch on Sunday and he talked for two hours - such interesting revelations that I made a précis of them for Sir Henry which has been sent home with his dispatch. When Roddolo left, Ken and I went out shooting in the gardens above the town and consulted together. He and Iltyd came to dinner to meet the 3 Commissioners. The President is Mr de Wirsén, a Swede, honest, fat and unintelligent. The live wire is Count Teleki, a Hungarian - he is also the danger. The third is Col. Paulis, a Belgian, half way between the two others in intelligence and well meaning. We had an extremely interesting evening. We kept far away from Iraq questions - we talked of archaeology, geography, anything you pleased - Teleki, who is a professor of some sort, taking eager part. Presently, after dinner, de Wirsén and Paulis began putting us questions, quite honest questions which we could answer very easily and were glad to answer. Ken and Iltyd played up beautifully. But Teleki, as soon as the talk turned on the Iraq, lost all interest. He never questioned, he never commented; it was as if he didn't want to know anything. It was very striking we all felt.

Document 7c

[28 October 1925]
Baghdad, Oct. 28

....

The Laidoner party arrived on Monday morning in heavy rain after having a forced landing in the desert and spending the night there. The rain had not begun till day break and they seemed to have regarded the whole episode as an interesting experience. H.E. made me stay to lunch to help with their entertainment. I like Laidoner. He is a large stolid Estonian who speaks no known language but French and that with a total disregard for genders, subjunctives, and all the grosser and finer nuances. This does not discompose him at all. He goes on as calmly as a tank and rolls the French tongue flat. He has an odd looking, rather Mongolian, Cheko-Slovak colleague called Jač (pronounced Yacks) who has the highest opinion of British methods, a good beginning, and a larger-than-life secretary who speaks English and is very friendly. A pleasant Spaniard, named Ortega, and a little grig of a Swiss, Charršre, a secretary of the League, complete the party. Charršre was here with the Frontier Commission and will now, I think, find himself in a very different entourage. I feel that it is scarcely to be regretted that the most bloodcurdling accounts of the state of the refugees and the atrocities of the Turks are now pouring in. These Laidoner will be able to verify for himself. He goes to Mosul on Friday.

Document 7d

[25 November 1925]
Baghdad, Nov. 25

....

On Monday afternoon Sylvia went out with Mr Keeling. I was feeling very tired so I telephoned to Ken to take me out in his car for an hour before sunset, which he did. It was restful. He also took us to the palace to dinner - a big dinner to say goodbye to Sir Henry. There were no surprises for me about my dinner partners for I had arranged the table that morning with the King's ADC Tahsin Beg (who dined with us in London, you remember.) I sat between the P.M. whom I love and Mr Cooke's Minister, Hamdi Beg with whom I also get on very well. Sylvia I put by the A.V.M. so that those two were happy. We did not stay long after dinner as H.E. was leaving at 6 a.m. Oh I must tell you that Laidoner has come back and goes tomorrow straight to the Council of the League with his tale. He leaves Col. Jač (prononc, Yaksh) at Mosul to keep watch. Laidoner came to tea yesterday (Thursday) with one of the League officials, M. Charršre, a Swiss. (Charršre made a bad entry. First he stepped on my little dog who howled; then he shook me so hard by the hand that I nearly howled too.) Laidoner says that there are no words in any language to express the plight of the refugees who fled from the Turks. I hope he will find some words in which to tell the Council about it and that they will be so impressive that the Council will overlook his talking *un jeune fille and une vieillard* [a young girl and an old man].

COLLECTION OF DOCUMENTS 8

British House of Commons and House of Lords Hansards

Document 8a

MASSACRE OF CHRISTIANS
HC Deb 14 December 1925 vol 189 cc950 - 2

Mr. T. P. O'CONNOR (by Private Notice)
asked the Under - Secretary of State for the Colonies if the report of General Laidoner with reference to the massacre and deportation of Nestorian Christians in and around Mosul will be published as a White Paper before the Debate on Iraq this week; and if there can be embodied in the same White Paper the Official Reports from our own representatives, and also a full Report with regard to the later massacres and deportations of Chaldeans, as set forth in the letter of Sir Henry Dobbs, Commissioner for Iraq?

Mr. ORMSBY - GORE
I only received notice of the hon. Member's question at half - past one, when I made inquiries in the Department. It appears that General Laidoner's Report was only present at Geneva last Friday, and has not yet readied the Department. I am afraid that even if it does reach the Department to - night there will not be time to have it printed in the form of a White Paper by Thursday.

Lieut. - Commander KENWORTHY
How is it that this Report appeared in Press several days ago and yet the Colonial Office have not got it?

Mr. ORMSBY - GORE
The Report was made not to the British Government but to the Council of the League of Nations, and handed to them at Geneva last

Friday. It will, no doubt, be sent on by the Secretariat of the League of Nations in due course, but official procedure is sometimes a little slower than Press telegrams.

Mr. CLYNES
In view of the great human issues raised in the question, will my hon. Friend endeavour to do his best to get this White Paper in time for the Debate on Thursday?

Mr. ORMSBY - GORE
I will certainly make inquiries. I believe it is the intention of my right hon. Friend the Secretary of State, if possible, to return from Geneva for the purposes of the Debate, and he, no doubt, will have all the latest information which he has received at Geneva regarding the occurrences which have taken place. I cannot say more.

Lieut. - Commander KENWORTHY
With regard to these occurrences, can the hon. Member state whether his right hon. Friend at Geneva, the Secretary of State for the Colonies, is in fact negotiating direct with the Turkish Delegates; and, if so, will questions of the safety of the remaining Christians be one of the subjects under discussion?

Mr. ORMSBY - GORE
I am afraid that question does not arise out of the original question, and I must ask my hon. and gallant Friend to put it down.

Mr. O'CONNOR
As the information contained in this report is of vital importance, especially in view of the fact that the latest massacres and deportations took place in September of this year, just at the very moment when Mosul was under discussion, and that these massacres and deportations were strenuously denied by the Turks, may I put it to the hon. Gentleman that by telegram or otherwise we should be in possession of this report before we discuss the future of Iraq?

Mr. ORMSBY - GORE
What I will endeavour to do is, if it is being printed, as I believe it is, at Geneva, to obtain copies of the Geneva prints (which think will be in the French and English languages), even if we cannot reprint it here. I will make inquiries with that object at once. I do not think I can say more. The pressure on the printing stall of the Government is consid-

erable, and I fancy that the report of General Laidoner is rather a full report.

Mr. THURTLE

Is the hon. Gentleman quite satisfied that these reports about massacres in Iraq have not been coloured for propaganda purposes by these concerned?

Mr. ORMSBY - GORE

Yes, Sir; I am quite satisfied that the official representative of the League, sent out under the auspices of the League, cannot and ought not to be accused in that way.

Document 8b

LEAGUE OF NATIONS
HL Deb 21 December 1925 vol 62 cc1679 – 706

LORD PARMOOR rose to call attention to the Council meeting at Geneva, and to move for Papers. The noble and learned Lord said: My Lords, I have indicated to the noble Viscount who is going to reply to my Question that I want to call attention to two specific matters. So much is now being done at each meeting of the Council of the League of Nations that it really is impossible on one occasion even briefly to consider all the points which may arise. The two matters to which I have given him notice that it is my intention to call his attention are the questions of Mosul and disarmament, and I have also given him an indication of the class of points that I am likely to raise, so that he may be fortified in giving the reply of the Government.

The first, question that I want to deal with is that of Mosul. This is a question of extreme immediate importance. There is a suggestion that we may come under an obligation that will be in operation for a period of twenty - five years regarding the frontier between Iraq and Turkey. We have to recollect in this matter - and I shall have to call your Lordships' attention to one or two phrases in the Covenant of the League of Nations - that Great Britain is not acting on her own behalf or for her own advantage, but as a Mandatory, as a representative of the League of Nations under Article 22 of the Covenant. Her first duty as a Mandatory is to provide as far as possible for the good government, security and peace of the people who are placed under her charge - in this case the people of Iraq, who live to the south of the frontier line which is now being laid down as the proper boundary between Iraq and Turkey, by the Council of the League.

The first point that I wish to make is this. I do not think that this good government and security can be attained in a district of this character unless there is good will and friendliness between this country and Turkey. I shall have to call attention later to the Report of General Laidoner, who has shown quite conclusively that some of the evils of which he specially complains have taken place north of the line, and therefore in the territory which will be left within the sovereignty of Turkey. I shall have to come back to this point a little later and a little more in detail, but it appears to me that no protection can be given to the people called the Nestorian or Assyrian Christians that can really be effective unless Turkey and Great Britain can co - operate together in a kindly and friendly spirit.

....

That position, I think, is emphasised in this case by the Report which was made by General Laidoner which was lately laid before the Council of the League at Geneva. He dealt with four matters. In the first place he pointed out that this was a wild region where there were constant tribal wars, where everyone went about armed and the different tribal or village chiefs were in a condition of almost constant warfare. He said that those conditions would probably be more or less continuous, and he threw no blame for them upon either Turkey or Great Britain. He then referred to the question of the occupation of certain villages by Turkish military posts and patrols, and also to the allegation that flights had been made over the frontier line by British aircraft. Neither of those matters did he consider of importance. He said that at present the frontier line was undefined and not marked out, and that instances of that kind might he expected but the fourth point to which he called attention was a point of extreme importance in his view.

That was the deportation of Christians from points north of the proposed line to the south of the proposed line, within the territory to be adjudicated to Iraq. The history of those deportations is very terrible to read. No one doubts the horrors to which General Laidoner refers. They are further emphasised by the report of his own staff, who personally investigated the condition of these deported Christians, and I may take it - I am sure I should not make any other statement - that it is of extreme importance to our national honour, and the responsibilities that we have undertaken, that we should do all in our power to prevent such horrors from being enacted in the future. But then comes the question, how is that to be done? After all, those Christians, who I see were denounced as "traitorous brigands" from the Turkish point of view, cannot be immediately under our jurisdiction and sovereignty. They are outside the line which from the end of this year, or whatever the date may be, would be the frontier line between Iraq and Turkey.

How can we deal with a difficulty of this kind? I said at the outset, and I want to emphasise it again, that it can only be dealt with satisfactorily by friendly arrangement between Great Britain and Turkey. The alternative is really to consign these Christians on the north side of the line to Turkish horrors, probably aggravated because they are regarded as a traitorous element in the Turkish Republic.

....

LORD PARMOOR

The only suggestion which could possibly have been raised was the form of it.

VISCOUNT CECIL OF CHELWOOD

Oh, no. There is no limit to the questions which any Member of the League may raise before the Council of the League. But what are the actual changes, looking at it as an international matter, which would justify a change of policy on the part of the Government? There has been a certain amount of Turkish pressure, and I am not saying a word which could embitter or envenom any controversy we may have with the Government of Turkey. But no doubt there has been pressure.

In addition, we have had the Report of General Laidoner. I do not quite agree with the noble Lord's estimate of the importance of that Report. It is not a question of what is going on in the district from which these unhappy refugees came. That, I agree, is beyond our competence to deal with. It is a question of what may happen if we abandon our trust over the district which we at present administer. The noble Lord referred to certain passages in General Laidoner's Report in which he spoke of the disturbed condition of the district from which these refugees came. I had the advantage of considerable conversation with General Laidoner after he had made his Report, and he was equally strong in praise of the striking difference in the districts over which we exercised a mandatory influence. He reported in the strongest terms that conditions are absolutely stable and peaceful. I remember that he gave me an illustration in the fact that even the highest officials could walk about without any armed guard or police to look after them - a condition of affairs which, he said, was not always to be found even in the more civilised States.

In dealing with the policy of abandonment, if I may so term it, we must recognise and face the fact that, if we go out, we shall inevitably be considered to be going out in obedience to pressure from Turkey and we shall run a grave risk of seeing, when we have gone out, an emigration which the General himself put at tens of thousands - 60,000 or 90,000 persons was his estimate of the population that would not be content to remain in the district. That is a very serious state of things to contemplate. And that is not the only thing. The Council's Commission, presided over by the Swedish gentleman, M. de Wirsén, who went out to investigate, reported that the present frontier, the Brussels line, was a perfectly good frontier from the point of view of defence, if defence became necessary, and that, whenever you went back, you would have a frontier that gradually got worse the further back you went, because the slope goes down and becomes more and more deficient in natural obstacles. Accordingly, if you went back, you would have a worse country, that is a more expensive country to defend, if defence became necessary. You would also have less resources, because it happens that normally the territories to the north are some of the richest in production in the whole territory of Iraq. So far, therefore, as we should remain responsible for the defence of Iraq, our position would be more expensive with less resources with which to meet it.

Then we should have to face the refugee problem that might come upon us - that, according to this very competent judge, would come upon us. I do not know whether it is realised how small a proportion of the population of the Vilayet of Mosul is Turkish. The proportion is about five per cent. The majority of the population are Kurdish, and next to them come Arabs - both, it is true, Mussulmans, but not especially acceptable to the strong Nationalist Turkish sentiment which prevails in Turkey at the present moment. Then come the Christians - there are, if I remember rightly, some 60,000 of them - then the Turks, who number, I think, some 40,000, and then smaller bodies of Yezidis, Jews and others. I do not, of course, know how many of those would become refugees, but I cannot reject the strong possibility that a large proportion of them would be refugees under conditions of the greatest horror, if some of the scenes were repeated that have occurred already. I am sure that no one - can have read the Report of General Laidoner's assistants without feeling how terrible has been the lot of the refugees there described. As I have said, we should have less resources and greater demands upon us in meeting whatever responsibility lay upon us with reference to these matters.

I do not want to put the thing too high, but I cannot help feeling that a policy of abandonment of that kind would, in the existing circumstances and after everything that has occurred, be a serious blow to our reputation and one that would have a repercussion in other countries far removed from Mesopotamia. Finally - I do not want to put the thing in a sentimental or excessive statement - it does seem to me a policy which I should have the greatest difficulty in supporting, if we are to desert those who have, at our invitation and at our instigation, declared themselves our friends and, per se, declared themselves as the possible enemies of any of those who might come after us. I do think that a Government that deserts its friends, the subjects who have trusted us, is committing one of the very worst crimes which a Government can possibly commit.

That is the policy of abandonment. But there is, in terms at any rate, quite a different policy that is sometimes recommended. It is a minor policy, and I am not quite sure whether it is the policy which the noble Lord recommends. I refer to the policy of refusing to undertake to make a Treaty to give the pledge that the Council asks for.

LORD PARMOOR
Hear, hear.
....

LORD PARMOOR

My Lords, I thank the noble Viscount for the answer he has given on both the points which I raised. On the disarmament point I only desire to say this, that presumed comprehensiveness in one sense leads to impracticability, if not impossibility, and that is what I fear from the form of comprehensiveness to which the noble Viscount referred. At the same time I will corroborate his view that technical difficulties are really only obstacles so long as there is not an earnest desire on the part of various peoples to carry out a reduction of armaments, and that so soon as a general desire of that kind is really entertained, these technical objections are likely to disappear.

The more important point I want to say a few words about is what the noble Viscount said with regard to Mosul. I do not think that he at any rate fully understood the point I made, and I want to make it quite clear, so that there may be no misunderstanding. Of course I agree with him that the decision of the Council as an arbitral body must be implemented by the action of the British Government. There is no question between us on that point. But the particular matter to which I called attention - namely, the period of twenty - five years - was not submitted to the arbitral decision and is not dealt with as part of the arbitral decision. The arbitral decision was given as to the direction of the frontier line and that was the only matter which, under the Treaty of Lausanne, was referred to the decision of the Council of the League. The British Government is invited to submit a new treaty for twenty - five years.

VISCOUNT CECIL OF CHELWOOD

They go on to say that their award will not be definitive until that has been done.

LORD PARMOOR

That is a condition which in my view cannot be attached to the award as an arbitral decision. The arbitral decision is the decision of the frontier line; the invitation to accept a Mandate of twenty - five years is an invitation only. I do not want, however, to bandy technical points with the noble Viscount. I do think that a new Mandate of twenty - five years is a most serious matter. I agree with him that you cannot accept a Mandate of this kind without creating responsibilities towards the mandated country and under the conditions prevailing in Iraq, if you remain there for twenty - five years you will find that obligations and responsibilities are undertaken that will make it practically impossible for you with national honour to leave Iraq at all. Does the noble Viscount really think that, if we accept this period of twenty - five years as a maximum, there is the remotest chance of Great Britain's resigning the Mandate in a shorter period?

VISCOUNT CECIL OF CHELWOOD

Certainly. I thought I had said in the plainest possible language that it is twenty - five years, or the period within which Iraq shall be in a position to apply for membership in the League of Nations, which we have said we will forward to the utmost of our power. It is quite true that, if Iraq were to remain in exactly the same position as she is in now, and we were to remain in exactly the same position as we are in now, we should evidently be no further advanced at the end of twenty - five years, but our policy is to avoid that happening, by enabling Iraq to stand by herself, and by coming to a friendly arrangement with Turkey, which will render the burdensome nature of our position, such as it is, either nonexistent or very much less.

LORD PARMOOR

That is a matter upon which it is possible to have differences of opinion, but it is not the point which I am stressing. In fact, it has nothing to do with it. What I say is that the longer you stay under the conditions of a Mandatory responsible for the administrative Government of Iraq, the stronger will almost certainly be the argument that you cannot leave Iraq, because, in proportion to the length of time that you maintain your administrative position, will be the growth of fresh responsibilities which national honour will compel us to undertake. That is the whole point. The people of Iraq were given notice in the original Mandate that we would only be responsible for four years. Well, apparently we differ upon that. I say it is perfectly clear to any one who reads the original Mandate that we were only to be responsible for four years, and that if, at the end of the four years, Iraq was not sufficiently grown up to be a Member of the League of Nations, then the matter was to be reconsidered. I attach the very greatest importance to the limitation introduced in the original Mandate. If the noble Viscount is right, there ought to be no period now inserted at all. You ought merely to wait until, with the passage of time, Iraq is in a position to stand by itself. No other consideration arises except that - certainly no consideration of time. Immediately you introduce a period such as twenty - five years you come under an obligation which at the end of that time will imply an almost permanent obligation. That has been the history of other places - not under Mandates, because the history of Mandates is a new principle.

You can approach a Mandate from two points of view. One is with the idea of getting rid of it by educating the mandated people as quickly as possible, the other is to take the point of view of saying: "We do not want to leave. We are here promoting interests which we cannot abandon, having regard to our ideas of national honour." That is the wrong way of looking at the position of a mandated territory. And it is for that reason that I think it is a fatal mistake, in dealing with such a vital issue, to come under any obligation which can be construed, and which I think will be construed, as making us responsible for Iraq for at least a period of twenty - five years.

The noble Viscount, I think, hardly realises the nature of the obligation which we are undertaking for this long time. Suppose we cannot come to a friendly arrangement with Turkey - which the noble Viscount knows, perhaps better than I do, is not an easy matter: What is to be the result? How long are we to remain under an obligation if Turkey does not adopt a friendly attitude? What will be the cost of military, naval, and air expenditure? I quite agree that, when you put yourselves into a position of that kind, you cannot leave the people towards whom you have undertaken responsibilities without fulfilling those responsibilities as a matter of national honour and national prestige. I am not at all reassured by what the noble Viscount has said, and I believe that there is a strong feeling in all Parties in this country - we know it prevails in the Conservative Party - that no such obligation, of practically a permanent kind, ought to be undertaken, at least until the feeling of the country has been ascertained.

Motion, by leave, withdrawn.

Document 8c

MESOPOTAMIA
(DEPORTATION OF CHRISTIANS)

HC Deb 23 February 1926 vol 192 cc306 - 7

Mr. SCRYMGEOUR
asked the Secretary of State for Foreign Affairs whether reports have reached him as to atrocities perpetrated by certain Turkish regiments upon Christians on the northern border of the British mandate territory of Iraq; if so, whether he is taking up the matter with the League of Nations; and, if not, whether he will make inquiries with a view to definite representations being made in the proper quarter?

The UNDER - SECRETARY of STATE for FOREIGN AFFAIRS (Mr. Godfrey Locker - Lampson)
Information reached His Majesty's Government early in September last to the effect that the Turkish authorities were deporting large bodies of Christians from the districts to the north of the so - called Brussels line, and that these deportations were being carried out in circumstances of great cruelty. This information was brought by His Majesty's Government to the notice of the League of Nations on the 21st September, and, as a result, a Commission was sent out under General Laidoner to investigate the matter on the spot. Its reports were made to the Council of the League, and have been published as Command papers Nos. 2557 and 2563.

Mr. SCRYMGEOUR
Do I understand that representations will be made to the League of Nations to expedite action to prevent further atrocities?

Mr. LOCKER - LAMPSON
Since the investigation was made we have had no information at all that any further deportations have taken place.

Sir H. BRITTAIN
Is it not the case that, notwithstanding these atrocities, the Prohibitionist party last week voted against the Iraq Treaty?

COLLECTION OF DOCUMENTS 9
ARTICLES FROM THE TIMES

Document 9a

15 September 1924

The Iraqi Frontier
Turkish Vali's Capture
FROM OUR CORRESPONDENT
BAGHDAD, SEP. 4 (by mail)

Considerable interest has been aroused here by the announcement that the Turks have decided to lay their case for the inclusion of Mosul in Turkey before the Assembly of the League of Nations. In the meantime an incident, recently occurred in the Hakkari country, on the Northern frontier, which illustrates the kind of thing which is likely to be continually happening should any part of the Assyrian country be subjected to Turkish rule.

It appears that Halil Rifaat Bey, the Turkish Vali of Hakkari, was touring in the mountainous no-man's land between Julamerk and Chal, immediately north of the present administrative boundary of Iraq. He unwisely attempted to make capital out of his tour for propaganda purposes, and the impression was created that the Vali was marching to Chal at the head of a large force with the object of forcibly subduing the Assyrian tribes of that neighbourhood. Even more unwisely, the Vali actually ventured into the country of the Tkhuma, one of the most warlike of the Assyrian tribes, with an escort of only a few gendarmes.

In the meantime the trans-frontier Assyrians had sent an appeal for help to the Iraqi authorities at Amadia, to whom-they are not unnaturally inclined to look for protection. A very proper reply was sent to them by the local *Qaymaqam* warning them against taking any offensive action against the Vali, who was not credited with any hostile intentions. Before these instructions had reached their destination the inevitable had happened; the Vali's escort came into collision with the Tkhuma. Each side naturally accuses the other of having fired the first shot, but in any case a skirmish ensued in which the Turks were outnumbered, and most of them, including Vali Rifaat Bey himself, were taken prisoner and their baggage looted. The Vali was taken by his captors, not to Baghdad as reported from Constantinople, but across the frontier to an Assyrian Malik[116] within Iraqi territory. The latter, who as it happened had received the instructions from Amadia, showed them to the Tkhuma tribesmen and persuaded them to release their prisoners and to send them back to Julamerk.

When news of the incident reached Mosul the Admini-strative Inspector went at once to Amadia to arrange for the release of Vali Rifaat Bey, only to find that he had been released already. Knowing, as we do, that the local government officials not only acted with scrupulous correctness throughout, but that they even attempted to dissuade the trans frontier Assyrians (for whose actions they cannot be held responsible) from taking hostile action against the Vali, we may learn several instructive lessons from this incident, viz.:-

1. The Assyrians whose habitat is to the north of the boundary at present adopted for administrative purposes look to the Iraqi Government as their natural protector.

2. The Assyrians, having thrown in their lot with the Allies against the Turks in the war, will never again tolerate the presence of Turkish officials in their midst or any attempt by the Turks to administer their country.

3. Turkish officials hold the Iraqi Government responsible for the conduct of the Assyrian tribes in the Hakkari country which the Turkish Government claims to control. In fact, the whole significance of this incident so strikingly supports the British case for the inclusion of the Hakkari country in Iraq that the Turks may be partially excused for saying that it is deliberately stage-managed by the Iraqi Government. There is no other way open to them of explaining away a piece of evidence which is so damning to their case.

---

116. Assyrian chieftain.

Document 9b

30 September 1924
The Turkish Raids Into Iraq
Intrigues Among the Kurds

No news of any further development of the situation to the north of Amadia has reached London, but it is now known that most of the Turkish Regular troops who crossed the Iraqi boundary were dispatched from the frontier garrison town of Gezira and form part of Jevad Pasha's army corps, the headquarters of which are at Amida [Diarbekir]. The peace strength of this army corps probably does not exceed 11,000 men, and no indications of any mobilization appear to have been observed. The movement seems to have been accompanied by an incursion into the Assyrian territory, to which the Turkish authorities recently sent a governor, who was forcibly expelled. This action on their part was, in the opinion of the Foreign Office, a breach of Article 3 of the Treaty of Lausanne, which provided that no military or other movement should take place which might modify the status quo from July 24, 1923, in all disputed areas on the Turco-Iraq frontier.

The Assyrian territory in question was at the time administered by neither British nor Turkish officials, but by the tribal councils of the Assyrians, who had returned thither in 1921. Shortly after the signature of the Treaty the Angora Government proposed to send a Governor there. His Majesty's Government protested and nothing further having been heard of the matter it was naturally presumed that the Turks accepted the British stand- point. In June, however, the attempt to install a Governor had the effect which Angora doubtless anticipated. While no massacres have been reported, there is reason to believe that the villages which the Assyrians who returned to their homes in 1921 had rebuilt have been burnt and pillaged, and the refugee problem has thus been revived in an acute form by the action of the Turks, who obviously are bent upon expelling all Assyrians from their territory, which they hope to acquire. There are also indications that the Angora Government hopes to cause internal disturbances in Kurdish Iraq, in order to be able to assert at Geneva that the inhabitants of the Amadia District are discontented with the present regime.

Document 9c

8 October 1924

Turkish Propaganda
(FROM OUR OWN CORRESPONDENT)
CONSTANTINOPLE, OCT. 7

There is a complaint in this morning's Tanin against the silence maintained in Angora about the question of Mosul and on Turkish foreign policy generally, and a contrast is drawn between the freedom enjoyed by the British Press and the local state of affairs. This complaint is, perhaps, somewhat belated, because the Turkish Press is now re- porting more freely versions of the frontier incidents and space is being given to propaganda and such statements as that attributed to the Kurdish chief Simko that if Mosul were not given to the Turks he would regard it as his duty to drench its streets, with blood. At the same time the telegrams published to-day seem to suggest that the Turks intend to become quieter. It is alleged that all military operations have come to an end with the flight across the Iraqi frontier of the Assyrians, and General Kazim Pasha, the Vekil of Defence, who arrived here yesterday, has insisted that the Turkish measures are of a purely internal nature.

Simko is the Kurdish chief who in October, 1921, raided Sawuj-Bulak in Persia and there cruelly ill-treated a number of American missionaries and shot some 500 Persian gendarmes who bad surrendered to him. He made himself a nuisance in the district until August, 1922, when he was defeated by Persian troops, who captured his stronghold, after which he withdrew into Turkish Kurdistan.

Document 9d

13 October 1924

Turks' Invasion Of Iraq
British Ultimatum
Imperial and Foreign News

After every possible opportunity had been given to the Turkish Government to reconsider its position and to amend its attitude in connexion with the invasion of British mandated territory in Iraq, Mr. Lindsay, the British diplomatic representative in Constantinople, last Thursday handed in a further Note to the Turkish Government. This communication can be described as an ultimatum, because it contained a demand for a withdrawal of the Turkish troops from the territory under our jurisdiction by noon last Saturday. The British Government warned the Turkish Government that if this demand were not complied with military action was inevitable. The Turkish Government, which made no reply to the previous and quite friendly British Notes addressed to it on this subject, has at last answered. It is probable, however, that the contents of this communication will not be found quite satisfactory.

The Note, which is couched in conciliatory language, avoids the main issue, and in it the Turkish Government takes up the attitude of injured innocence and pretends that no infringement of the rights of the British Government as mandatory of Iraq under the League of Nations has taken place - this under the pretext that although Turkish troops have entered the territory of the old vilayet of Mosul they have not crossed the line of effective British military occupation, as marked by the posts in Bir-Sivi, Banona, and Chaqallo.

As to the punitive expedition against the Assyrians, the Turkish Government claims that it was undertaken openly and with due warning to the local British authorities. The object of the expedition having been attained, the main forces of the expedition have been withdrawn, and there is no intention to enlarge the zone of occupation. The Turkish Government suggests that its attitude conforms exactly to the terms of the Treaty of Lausanne and it repeats that it is its firm intention to abide by them. The British Government, while recognizing the conciliatory tone of the Turkish answer, will probably not be able to accept it as satisfactory or final, as Turkish promises to abide by the decision of the Council of the League of Nations have been made on repeated occasions, but their sincerity still remains to be proved, all the more so because it is known that the Government of Angora has expressed its disapproval to Fethi Bey, the Turkish representative in Geneva, of his conciliatory attitude on the question of the frontier of Iraq.

THE BOUNDARY DISPUTE

The trouble on the northern frontier of Iraq is of long standing. The situation there is governed by the Treaty of Lausanne, which in Clause 2 of Article III. lays down:- The frontier between Turkey and Iraq shall be laid down in friendly arrangement to be concluded between Turkey and Great Britain within nine months. In the event of no agreement being reached between the two Governments within the time mentioned the dispute shall be referred to the Council of the League of Nations. The Turkish and British Governments reciprocally undertake that, pending the decision to be reached on the subject of the frontier, no military or other movement shall take place which might modify in any way the present state of the territories of which the final fate will depend upon that decision. On the map on this page is shown the area affected by the present invasion of Turkish troops. As the British and Turkish Governments were unable to reach the understanding stipulated in the Treaty of Lausanne, owing to the break-down of the direct negotiations in Constantinople on June 5 of this year, the frontier between Turkey and Iraq must be determined by the decision of the Council of the League of Nations, which is still pending.

Meanwhile, the temporary line of demarcation is defined by the words in clause 2 of Article III. of the Treaty, "present state of the territories." The meaning of these words is held by the Foreign Office to refer to the effective occupation of territories by the military and administrative authorities of the respective Governments on the day of the signature of the Treaty of Lausanne. The Turks appear to dispute this contention on the ground that at the time of the signature of the Armistice of Mudros on October 30, 1918, the British army in the Mosul area, under the command of Major-General Sir William Marshall, had barely reached a line roughly running just to the north of Mosul and to the south of Amadia, and that in a local arrangement with the commander of the Turkish forces in that area for the cessation of hostilities that line was accepted as the line of demarcation.

The British Government does not accept this argument, as it contends that any temporary arrangement which may have been made in October, 1918, between the local military commanders was necessarily superseded by the final agreement contained in the Treaty of Lausanne in 1923, and by that time British occupation had certainly and indisputably become effective within the whole area of the old Turkish vilayet of Mosul and had also been extended to the territory of the Assyrian tribes beyond it (the hatched area shown on the map).

TURKISH VALI'S ADVENTURE

This territory, which before the war had never been really under effective Turkish Government, had been resettled by the Assyrians who had fled from it when the Russians, with whom they had allied themselves, retreated from Van in 1917. After the Armistice the Assyrians gradually returned to their villages, and British administrative officers and police went into the area to preserve law and order. This state of affairs was not challenged by the Turks until October last year. At that time the British authorities in Mosul were informed that the Turkish Vali of Julamerk intended to cross the, main chain into Assyrian territory and to collect tribute from a Kurdish chieftain at Chal. This petty chief, or rather brigand, had, so the Turks contended, always been tributary to them before the war, receiving in reward the title of Mudir. The Turkish Government was warned without delay that the territory which the Vali intended to visit was in effective British occupation and that, therefore, under the terms of the Treaty of Lausanne, he would not be admitted. For some months after that nothing more was heard of the enterprise. At last, at the beginning of August, the Vali, Halil Rifaat Bey, in spite of the British warning, crossed the mountains with a small escort and appeared at the village of Hani, on the border of the Assyrian country. There he was met by armed Assyrians, who, after a short skirmish, took him prisoner and later sent him back over the border. This incident was brought to the notice of the Turkish delegates at Geneva and the warning against an unwarranted intrusion on British territory was repeated. The Turkish Government, however, ordered a punitive expedition to be sent against the Assyrians.

THE TURKISH INVASION

The country is extremely mountainous, and the pass from Julamerk over the main chain is difficult to negotiate for cavalry and artillery. Therefore, while a small column set out from Julamerk itself, the main force of the Turkish punitive expedition set out from its headquarters at Gezira, on the Tigris, to Rabanki, on the River Hazil, where it crossed into what is indisputably the territory of the old Mosul Vilayet. The country is held by the British only with a few police posts of native Iraqi Levies and patrolled by aeroplanes from the squadron stationed at Mosul. The Turkish force, after crossing the river, took the road towards Challek, a village where there is a bridge over the River Khabur. The Iraqi police had to retire, but two aeroplanes on patrol, coming up with the Turks on the road from Rabanki on September 14, bombed the column and obliged it to retreat. But reinforcements pushed up from Gezira arrived, and the Turks resumed their advance. They established a base at Challek, and then crossed to Ashita, in the Assyrian country. From there they came down to Chal, on the southern boundary of the Assyrian country and only 12 miles from Amadia. The Turkish commanders cannot plead the excuse of ignorance, because two days before their movement across the Hazil began the Turkish authorities at Gezira had been warned in writing against invading British mandated territory, and a similar warning was addressed later direct to the Turkish commander at Chal. Meanwhile the Assyrians have fled in panic from the villages they had only just rebuilt. Thousands of them have arrived at Amadia, and even at Mosul, clamouring for British protection. The Turks, by crossing the Hazil at Rabanki and advancing to Challek, have broken into what is without doubt British mandated territory, and this action greatly transcended in importance their unjustifiable invasion of the Assyrian country.

Document 9e

24 February 1925

Commissioners At Mosul
A Difficult Task
(FROM OUR CORRESPONDENT)
MOSUL, FEB. 10 (by overland mail)

It is doubtful if any of the Commissions appointed by the League of Nations has ever been faced with so difficult a task as that with which the present Commission in Mosul is dealing. During its first week the Commission was able to make very few inquiries, as it had first to find some way out of the difficulty in which the Turkish Government had placed it by attaching to the staff of the Turkish Assessor two Iraqis, Nadhim Nafehizada of Kirkuk and Yuzbashi[117] Fattah of Suleimaniya, who had fled the country and joined the Turks when Sheikh Mahmud rebelled against the Iraqi Government. Against these two men there exists intense resentment in Mosul.

On February 6 the Commission, to avoid further delay, obtained a declaration from Jevad Pasha, the Turkish Assessor, that he, on behalf of himself and his Government, accepted full responsibility if any unfortunate incident resulted from any members of his party visiting the town without police escorts. By this time the Commission, either collectively or individually, had seen most of the important people and had visited a number of people of all classes in their homes. It had interviewed the leaders of the Mosul Defence Association, who arrived accompanied by a large procession of fervent Iraqis, banners, native music, and tumblers; it had heard the views of the Chaldean Patriarch and other Christian divines, and had tracked down to their homes those who were believed to be afraid to state openly that they wanted the Turks back.

In spite of the number and variety of people the Commissioners have seen they have not exhausted the possibilities of this interesting and bewildering vilayet. So various are the communities that exist here and so confusing are the local politics that it defies the genius of any sincere searcher after truth to know where to begin and, having begun, where to end. Apart from the Shebaks, the Turkomans, and the Kurds, they have yet to see the village Arabs and the Bedouin Shammar. In the town excitement still runs high. As the Turks stayed most of the week indoors there were no Turks or Iraqi traitors for the patriots to molest in the streets. The Commissioners had shown that they did not welcome large crowds either round their residence nor at their elbow when they walked abroad.

---

117. Captain; *yüzbaşı* in Turkish.

The only thing that remained for those eager spirits who felt that they must openly demonstrate their patriotism was to have a kind of heresy hunt and to discover which was the least loyal section of townsmen. Suspicion naturally fell in turn upon everybody. Those who had always kept aloof from politics and had therefore not very actively bestirred themselves on this occasion were warned by candid friends that their loyalty was in doubt. The only reply to such friendly hints was large subscriptions by the wealthy to the funds of the *Jam´iyat ul-Difa´ al Watan*, or the National Defence Association, and on the part of the poor vocal demonstrations of hatred of the Turks. Having kept alight their fervour by an examination of each other, worthy of the Cromwellian Puritans, the extreme Nationalists were ready, on Saturday, to deal with any member of the Turkish Delegation who might venture into the town. The unfortunate victim was Yuzbashi Fattah, who, after visiting a local hajji, was set upon by the crowd, but escaped before any harm was done to him. This same Turkish delegate had a similar experience on Monday, when, on leaving the public baths, he was recognized, but was rescued by the police before he had received worse injury than the contemptuous expectorations of a crowd of Moslems.

SIR HENRY DOBB'S VISIT

On Saturday, February 7, the High Commissioner, Sir Henry Dobbs, flew up from Baghdad. When the aeroplane arrived over the aerodrome, though flying very low, it could hardly be seen because of a thick snowstorm. In landing the machine was badly damaged, but fortunately neither passenger nor pilot was hurt. Though Sir Henry's visit was short, he had a long interview with the Commission, and also on Sunday met all the political leaders of Mosul, divines, merchants and notables. At the latter meeting the High Commissioner heard the complaints of the Moslawis, many of whom are incensed against the Commission because it had given a hearing to any pro-Turk witnesses at all. The High Commissioner explained that after spending five hours with the Commission that morning he was convinced that the Commission now realized that Mosul belonged to Iraq and was an Arab town.

He found that the Commission resented the prevailing spirit of excitement, and therefore he advised all present to cease demonstrations and to adopt a calm, confident attitude, and so prove to the Commission that the people were in no doubt about the strength and justice of their case. The Commission, his Excellency pointed out, was in a very delicate position. It had to make its inquiry from Mosul for convenience sake, and consequently was working in a district controlled by one of the parties to the dispute. Therefore it was only natural that they should try by all means in their power to show their impartiality. This might mean that they would search out for pro-Turkish opinions in order to show the Turks that they were not merely following the wishes of the Government of Iraq. The Moslawi Ashraf (recognized Descendants of the Prophet), the High Commissioner pointed out, should not feel this as a slight. He had explained to the Commission the danger of an uncritical acceptance of witnesses which might give equal weight to the evidence of influential upright men, and that of unprincipled men or of ex-convicts or of men who owed the Government large sums of money. The Commissioners had promised him to give an opportunity to Mr. Jardine, the British Assessor, to give his comments on the character of each witness. In case any person was under a misapprehension as to the motives of Great Britain, the High Commissioner reminded the notables that Great Britain stood by her Allies, and was determined to secure for Iraq complete independence and prosperity.

The reason why a British Assessor had been appointed and not an Iraqi was that at Lausanne, Constantinople, and Geneva the Turks had objected to Iraqi representatives, declaring that all Iraqis were Turkish subjects. In spite of the High Commissioner's advice to keep calm, a brawl occurred immediately after the meeting between a leader of the violent pro-Iraq party and a well-known Arab Hajji, suspected of pro-Turkish sentiments. The Hajji got a black eye and his assailant a wound in the hand from the Hajji's dagger. The local authorities promptly imprisoned them both, but the incident has created much feeling. The Chaldean Patriarch and other Christian leaders have announced their intention of writing to the Pope, to Cardinal Bounae, Cardinal Mercier, and all Catholic leaders imploring them to intervene with the League of Nations to save from the Turks the Christians of Mosul, who number 120,000 souls and, with the Christians of Syria and Palestine, are all that is left of the two million Christian subjects of the Ottoman Empire of 1914.

The Kurds of Zakho, Amadia, Dohuk and Agtan have formed branches of the National Defence Association and have added to the revenue of the telegraph department by deluging the Commission, the parent association in Mosul, and its branches elsewhere with declarations and exhortations.

Turkish encroachments north of Amadia have ceased. They are busy however sending into Iraq copies of a pamphlet by one Hashim Nahid which urges the Kurds to declare for the Turks. As this Hashim was formerly a subordinate tax-collector, a calling neither respected nor beloved, his appeal will have little effect even on the simple Kurd. Tomorrow the Commission will split up. Count Paul Telecki is going to Arbil and Colonel Paulis to Kirkuk. M. af Wirsén, the chairman, will remain in Mosul. The three Commissioners will separately tour the villages of these three centres. They will each be accompanied by Turkish and Iraqi experts and Colonel Paulis will also be assisted by Count Pourtales, one of the Secretaries. This rather unusual procedure for a Commission is rendered necessary by the extent of the area to be visited in the short time available. When the villages have been visited the Commission as a whole will visit Arbil and Kirkuk probably about the 22nd of this month and then return to Mosul and tour the whole frontier districts.

Document 9f

17 August 1925

The Mosul Report
Views In Affected Districts
Kurds Satisfaction
(FROM OUR CORRESPONDENT)
MOSUL, AUG. 15

As the local newspaper is not published daily, a summary of the recommendations of the Turco-Iraqi Frontier Commission was not published in Mosul until last Tuesday. The publication has not yet caused here any great excitement. This is partly due to the general belief which has grown that the present frontier would become permanent, and to a refusal to believe that Great Britain would hand back the inhabitants of Iraq to the mercy of the Turks. The lack of excitement is also due to the vagueness of the conditions and apparently to the illogical secondary solutions tacked on to the Commission's main conclusions.

The inhabitants of outside districts, including the Kurds and the Yezidis, have received the report with great satisfaction. They are confident that the conditions for ensuring their remaining in Iraq will be carried out. The Kurds are particularly pleased with the recommendations, which are to then an agreeable contrast to the present plight of the Kurds in Turkey, where the policy is apparently to blot out anything Kurdish, the execution of the Sheikh Abdul Qadir and the treatment of the religious Sheikhs having had a profound effect on the Mosul Kurds. The Christians and other mixed races and religions who inhabit the Mosul plain and foothills express relief, qualified by some anxiety, that the assistance of the League will be forthcoming.

As the Assyrians, however, can judge for themselves from the summary of the report, the Commission's findings still leave over for settlement the Nestorian Assyrian problem. The treatment of Christians in Turkey since the Treaty of Lausanne, and especially in the north of Zakho in the last few months, has been such as effectually to put a return to Turkey out of the question. Also, the present Kemalist Government has not shown any favourable disposition towards the idea of local autonomy for non-Turks as the Commission suggest. Naturally the intelligentsia of Mosul city have been readier with criticism than the people of the outer districts.

The Nationalists are indignant at the statement that the majority of the inhabitants of the Mosul vilayet would have preferred Turkish to Arab sovereignty if they knew League support was going to be withdrawn. Disappointment is expressed in the city that the Commission has not appreciated the new spirit of the Orient and the national spirit of Iraq. Failure on the part of the Commission to make more mention of this in the report is criticized almost as want of tact towards the policy of Great Britain as actually approved by the body which appointed the Commission. Apart from that, the moderate Nationalists do not resent the stipulation of 25 years of League assistance. They point out that when the Anglo-Iraq Treaty was passed the Assembly added a rider expressing the hope that Great Britain would defend the interests of Iraq on the northern frontier. The moderates are, however, afraid of the effect of Turkish propaganda upon the xenophobia of some of the extremists.

The two Iraqi outlaws who accompanied the Commission as Turkish experts were extremely unpopular in Iraq, and some sardonic glee is expressed that Suleymanie and Kirkuk whence these two hail, appear from the recommendations of the Commission safe to remain in Iraq, however unfavourable the League decision is. The statement of the Commission that legally the disputed territory belongs to Turkey has caused expressions of astonishment, especially as some of the inhabitants state that they were at the time told by the Commission that legally the disputed territory belonged to the League of Nations. The main conclusions, then, of the Commission have given satisfaction to the inhabitants as a whole, though certain of the subsidiary suggestions have aroused some comment. All Arabs, Kurds, and non-Moslems alike are anxiously looking to the League and to Great Britain to preserve for Iraq the strategic frontier which will allow her to live economically and politically, and the Assyrians still hope that the League and Great Britain will find a solution for their future security.

Document 9g

[17 September 1925]

Deportations Near Mosul, Plight of the Assyrians, Christians and Turks
(FROM OUR CORRESPONDENT)
Many of the Christian mountaineers in the disputed country to the north of Mosul, who have been driven from the neighbourhood of the Brussels line by a Turkish encircling movement, though Assyrians, belong to the Jacobite Church. They farm with their kinsmen the Nestorians and the Chaldeans of the plain, the Assyro-Chaldean nation whose destiny is to be decided at Geneva by the League.

The Jacobites and Chaldeans, who are less warlike and independent than the Nestorians, did not all actively participate in the general rising against the Turks during the war. A number of the Jacobites especially were able to hold their homes in the mountains until the recent comprehensive operations against the rebellious Sheikh Said brought 40,000 Regular troops into more or less permanent occupation of the frontier. Talk of a plebiscite under such conditions is a mockery.

The Jacobites are in no way connected with the better known adherents of the "Pretender." They are followers of a monk named Jacob the Beggar, who roved from centre to centre in the sixth century, stiffening opposition to the decrees of the Council of Chalcedon. Their hierarch claims to be lineally descended from the Patriarchate of Antioch, and are now in close communion with Rome. It is this branch of the Assyrians who have been driven from their homes in the Goyan into the wildest and most inhospitable country in the whole highlands of Kurdistan. Formerly it was inhabited by Moslem Kurd and Nestorian Assyrian, but since the withdrawal of the latter the lives of Christian travellers, once they have passed Sheranis Islam, the last outpost on the Brussels line, are not worth an hour's purchase. The sight of any unprotected infidel inspires the worst in every Kurd. "They are not men, they are beasts" were the words of a Christian mountaineer from Marga, one of the villages from which deportations are now taking place. "If we attempted to move further into the Hakkari we should be cut to pieces and two regiments would not recover our bodies." That was a few months ago.

HARRASSED BY KURDS
Is the Turk repeating the fiendish scheme of the Armenian deportations, by which the pick of a nation was disarmed, conscripted, and drafted into remote and sparsely populated districts under the excuse of "colonizing Mesopotamia?" The great majority were driven to death

on a march which was never intended to have any other ending. Armed Kurds were encouraged to rid the column, to massacre the men, and carry off the young women and children, to be brought up as Moslems and sold into Turkish harems. It is a problem to the wanderer in the neighbourhood of the debatable country how a Christian people have contrived to exist at all in the face of Turkish enmity and the depredations of the Kurds. Only an appreciation of the Assyrian national character can supply the clue.

The Assyrians claim to be of the same race as Sargon and Sennacherib. Living in the mountains as shepherds and quarrymen, they escaped extermination at the destruction of Nineveh. The typical features of the Assyrians in the British Museum bas-reliefs are encountered again and again in these remote mountains. The true Assyrian is never a huckster; the ancient tradition of arms is too deeply engrained. Unlike the Armenians, they have preserved their independence in their mountain fastnesses, owning only a nominal allegiance to the Sultans of Turkey. The majority of them are still shepherds; some of them are sought after as builders. Many of the commonest words in their language, the months of the year, the names of domestic animals, are the same as in the mural inscriptions of the ancient Assyrians. They are Knight-Templars of the mountains; builders with one hand on the trowel, the other on a short sword. Christianity was brought to them by Thaddeus, who founded the Armenian Church. They were forgotten by the Council of Nicaea, a position which was not unsatisfactory, since when Christendom and Saracen waged war, the Assyrians passed as people of no importance. Later, under the sway of the Khalifs of Baghdad, they had a wonderful history, sending their missions as far afield as Malabar and China. It was the ravages of Timur the Lame which reduced their Church to mediocrity.

BATTLING FOR EXISTENCE

They first definitely threw in their lot with the Allies in 1915 in response to an invitation from the Russians, who had pushed forward to Lake Van to relieve the victims of the Armenian massacres. Scarcely had they committed themselves when the Russians withdrew and left them to fight the Turks alone. Within five weeks of their decision they were battling for their lives. They fought a desperate action as far as Urmia, in which polyglot city they established their authority and created an asylum of refuge for thousands of fugitives from the sword of Islam.

In July, 1918, *liaison* was effected with a British flying column, and, despite fierce attacks by the 5th and 6th Turkish Divisions, they fought a rearguard action under General Agha Petros to join the main British forces in Mesopotamia. The long, straggling, ill-armed column was ha-

rassed by Kurds and Persians as they marched. Men were slaughtered by hundreds, women stripped and outraged, girls carried away to Musulman harems. It is a historical epic, as great as the retreat from Moscow.

Since then the work of the Assyrians in the building of the new Iraq has received scarcely any recognition. Without them the country lacks the stiffening of a fighting class. They have come forward in thousands to serve in the Levies and the police, where their soldierly qualities have won the unstinted praise of British officers. The tilt of their picturesque stetson hats, their simplicity and high spirits recall all the boyishness of the Gurkhas. They have the mountaineers' instinct for thrift; yet their hospitality and kindness are proverbial. It was their firm belief that under British protection they would speedily be put back in their own homes, with compensation for their losses in the war. But ill-advised agitation has rendered their plight to-day pitiable in the extreme.

Crowded as the majority of them are into the low-lying areas behind the Brussels line, there is only sun-shrivelled pasturage for their sheep. Their ambitions are centred in the higher mountains which were their homes. They are now in desperate straits; many of, them are starving, others are living in caves ... holes-in-the-ground. They have no diplomats to urge their case. Their hereditary Patriarch, Mar Shimun, was treacherously murdered by a Kurdish Agha, with whom, at the request of a political officer, he was endeavouring to arrange an alliance. The succession passed to a minor, at present being educated at St. Augustine's College, Canterbury. In his absence, his aunt, Surma Khanum d'Mar Shimun, bears the burdens of State. She is a grey-haired lady of infinite charm, who would grace an English home. Some of her more reckless subjects have called her nervous. Quaintly she recounts when she was living in the powder magazine at Urmia she refused to allow smoking when high explosive was distributed! But she admits to genuine nervousness now.

Apprehension for the future

Should the British relinquish Mosul there is nothing but retreat anew, this time into the wilderness. Often in the evenings at sunset she steals away to the grassy mounds which once were Nineveh, in utter helplessness and desolation of soul. Away in the distance are Qudshanis, Tyari, and Tkhuma, the lost homes of the nation. She is a pathetic figure standing there, alone and impotent, while thousands of her subjects are being marched to martyrdom. Geneva seems so very far away from Mosul.

Document 9h

[October 30, 1925]

Turks And Mosul Frontier
(FROM OUR CORRESPONDENT)
MOSUL, October. 29

I have just returned from a tour of the villages immediately south of the Brussels Line. Winter has set in early this year and there has been much rain.

The mountains on and to the north of the Brussels Line are already capped with snow, and the rivers, which this summer were lower than for many years past, have suddenly filled with chocolate hued torrents. The wretched beings who contrived to escape when the Christians were being deported by the Turks to Elki, the chilly mountain region 60 or 70 miles north-east of Zakho, report that snow fell upon them several times while they were being kept in the open without shelter or coverings. The nomads have come south and are entering Iraq, and their animals and herds are being examined by the veterinary officers of the Iraq Government lest they should have contracted serious infectious diseases while in Turkey.

These wanderers state that the Kurdish insurgents are still holding their own against the Turks in many areas, and that the Kurdish fugitives who were instigated by the Turks to flee over the frontier from Iraq are disgusted with the behaviour of the Turks towards the Kurds, and are anxious to reinstate themselves into the good graces of the Iraq Government. They state that while the Turks indulge in a certain amount of blustering talk about war, their troops are ill-equipped and discontented. From their reports it would appear that the Kurdish leaders of the Goyan district have published far and wide their disapproval of the deportation of the local Christians by the Turks.

ACORNS AS FOOD

The Nestorian Assyrians, who last autumn had to abandon their homes in the disputed territory in the Hakkari when they were threatened by the Turks who had entered Iraq behind them to the south-west, have now descended from the high pasturages where they had spent the summer and have come down into the valleys where the local Governor has divided them among the villages. The majority of these Assyrians are in urgent need of financial relief, and widows and orphans will certainly succumb this winter if no relief is forthcoming. Those settled among the foothills and in the lower valleys have not even forage for their sheep and plough cattle, many of which died during the hot summer owing to the drought and scarcity of pasture. On crossing the Khabur from the Amadia into the Zakho district a terrible sight awaits the traveller at Bir-Sivi, a Christian village some nine miles north-east of Zakho. Here are collected in rude temporary booths and in tents provided by the military those inhabitants of the villages of Upper Merga [Žor], Lower Merga [Žer], and Der-Shish who contrived to escape the deportations.

They barely escaped with their lives, and utterly lack possessions of any sort; they have no bedding, and some have only one garment to protect them from the weather, which is already very cold and wet. They were eating acorns when I saw them, and many were ill. The faces of many of the women bore that dull, fixed look which tells of overpowering despair. These poor people relate terrible stories of the atrocious callousness and barbarous brutality of the Turks, who, they say, put to death old men and old women or toddling babies because they could not keep up in the march. The women and girls, they declare, were taken away at nightfall by the Turkish guards and kept till morning. Seven girls were actually sold by Turkish soldiers to Kurds for money.

FACING STARVATION

The Iraqi Government is doing all it can to feed the fugitives, and the officers and men of the Royal Air Force and other units in Mosul have had a whip round and are sending money, old clothing, and wraps, but unless substantial help is forthcoming from Europe these Christians will scatter as beggars and gradually die off. In Zakho there are 2,000 others who managed to escape from the deportations. These are from the villages of Sinat, Baijo, Billo, Kuwalik, and Ser-e-Awrahe monastery. It is significant to notice that only men or very young children and old women have escaped; there are very few young women. Fugitives are still dribbling in, and the later arrivals report that the deportees from Baijo, Billo, Ser-e-Awrahe, Merga Žer, Merga Žor, and Muwalik were taken to Elki and there distributed among the villages of Kurdish chiefs, who had to give receipts for them.

They have no food of their own and receive little from their Kurdish or Turkish keepers, and many are dying of cold and starvation. No news has yet been received of where the inhabitants of Shuwait, Suli, and Nuzur were taken to, and northern villages such as Baz Alto, Hawuz Mayir, and Shi are being closely watched, though the Turks have not carried out their original intention of deporting them. The general feeling in the Mosul area, and especially in the frontier districts, is one of complete, almost pathetic, confidence in the British Government, and several Kurdish chiefs whose attitude was shaky a few months ago have now become loyal and helpful to the Iraqi Government.

THE BRUSSELS LINE

The Brussels Line (referred to in our Mosul Correspondent's despatch) is so called because it was laid down at a meeting of the Council of the League of Nations at Brussels in October of last year when considering the Mosul dispute. The Council then fixed in detail a frontier line showing the limit of the territories which might be occupied and ad- ministered by either aide until the establishment of the final frontier between Turkey and Iraq.

Document 9i

[11 December 1925]

Deportations At Mosul
(FROM OUR CORRESPONDENT)
MOSUL, Nov. 23

General Laidoner and one of the members of his Commission will leave Iraq shortly, in order to be present at the December session of the Council of the League of Nations. Part of the Commission, under Colonel Jack, remains in Mosul for the present. General Laidoner and the whole of his Commission have recently been staying at Zakho, where they carried out an inquiry among the 3,000 Christian refugees who managed to escape deportation by the Turks on the Brussels line. From the time the deportations began and the deportees were assembled at Elki up to the present moment refugees who managed to escape have been dribbling into Zakho in small parties. Many of these the Commission saw, and from them they inquired the conditions under which these wretched people were taken to Elki and detained there by the Turks. General Laidoner visited the village of Nuzur, near the Brussels line, which the Turks had occupied.

He also visited the mountains Simat and Der-Shish, two villages south of the Brussels line, from which the Christian inhabitants were expelled by the Turks. In a speech to the principal officials and notables of Mosul who assembled to wish him good-bye, General. Laidoner stated that he had been able to carry out his task in tranquility and he had thus been able- to arrive at an impartial and unexaggerated idea of what had happened. In his opinion the Iraq Government authorities were doing all they possibly could for the refugees at Zakho, whose condition was really serious. He congratulated the Iraqi Government authorities and the inhabitants on having evolved a condition of society in which all the various creeds and races were treated equally. Before leaving Mosul General Laidoner personally thanked all those who had assisted him or had been associated with him in the course of his inquiry. The Mutesarrif of Mosul expressed his appreciation of the great courtesy shown by General Laidoner to all the Iraqi Government officials and the interest taken by him in the working of their young state, and informed them of the eagerness of the officials to assist those members of the Commission who were staying behind in Mosul.

Document 9j

[11 December 1925]

Mosul Report At Geneva
Deportations by Turks
General Laidoner's Evidence
(FROM OUR. SPECIAL CORRESPONDENT)
GENEVA, DEC. 10

The Council met this morning to hear General Laidoner, who was commissioned by the League to investigate on the spot the report of Turkish violence against Christians on the Iraq border line. Circumstantial accounts of whole-sale deportations had been received in Geneva during the meeting of the Council in September, and these were to-day officially substantiated by the League Commissioner. When the proceedings began it was noticed that the Turkish delegates, as was perhaps natural in view of the business in hand, were not present.

A letter was read from them in which it was explained that the invitation to attend was only received at 11.30 last night, and that in any case, so long as the function of the Council was to operate in an arbitral capacity, the powers of the Turkish delegation must be regarded as suspended. Taking up the novel attitude of an expert on League procedure, the Turkish delegate then gave his opinion that the Council was not empowered by the Covenant to take decisions except by unanimous vote, including the interested parties, and supported his argument by reference to Articles 6 and 16.

After this diversion General Laidoner read his report, which was matter of fact but none the less impressive. He had not been allowed to go north of the Brussels Line by the Turks, but he had flown along that line in an aeroplane. In this connexion he mentioned that he judged that it was impossible from the ground to estimate by eye the exact position of an aeroplane nine or ten thousand feet up in a mountainous district; and he could give no opinion as to the Turkish charge that British aeroplanes had crossed the frontier. The Turks might have been genuinely misled by the fact that several villages generally supposed to be north of the Brussels Line were really the south of it. Some of these villages, notably Nezur, had been occupied by Turkish military posts. On maps Nezur was shown Ito [Alto] the north. In any case the local Turkish authorities had now been made acquainted with the true position of the boundary line, and the question of the violation of the frontier by either party might be regarded as settled.

"ATROCIOUS VIOLENCE"

All this was no excuse for the ruthless deportation and expulsion of Christians by the Turks which General Laidoner found had taken place and was still in progress when he left. In the district of Zakho there were 3,000 refugees, and every day isolated groups continued to arrive. They came chiefly from the zones between the Brussels Line and the frontier laid down by Great Britain. General Laidoner had satisfied himself beyond doubt that Turkish detachments under the command of officers occupied villages and first of all obtained delivery of all arms. They then imposed heavy fines and demanded women. Afterwards they pillaged the houses and subjected the inhabitants to atrocious and murderous acts of violence. The deportations were made en masse. Many of their victims died of starvation or cruelty. They had been unable to carry with them either food or clothing, and, therefore, the condition of deportees and refugees was pitiable. The Estonian General and his assistants had had many opportunities of getting into touch with refugees before they had been seen by anybody else, a fact to which he attaches importance in his report. The deportations, he considers, are still the cause of nervousness and unrest along the border and throughout the Vilayet of Mosul; the uneasiness has spread even to those Moslem inhabitants who favour the claim of Iraq. One of General Laidoner's conclusions is that the provisional frontier as fixed at Brussels is not the actual frontier. Certain parts of it are purely arbitrary; the present unsettled conditions in fact are most favourable to brigandage and tribal and village chiefs have no scruples about taking advantage of this state of things.

General Laidoner mentioned that a more detailed report on the evidence obtained was being drawn up and he was requested to lay this before the three members of the Sub-Committee. He was also asked to supply them personally with any explanations that they might require. General Laidoner is understood to have drawn from his visit the very definite conclusion that the whole population stands to lose enormously, by any substitution of Turkish for Anglo-Iraqi rule. He has referred with approval to the British administration and does not conceal his fears for the Christian communities should Great Britain give up her trusteeship. The Estonian General is a man of strong and independent character, and it is just possible that his evidence may have a decisive effect upon the deliberations of the subcommittee, which, as reported yesterday, cannot hope to attain a definite result of an arbitral nature unless unanimity be reached. The member of it who favours a compromised decision is understood to do so mainly on the ground that it would be unfortunate for a decision of the League in such a dispute to be given wholly in favour of a Great Power within the League against a small Power outside it. He may, in addition, have reasons on the merits of the case; but it has, anyhow, now been made clew by the League Commissioner's report that if consideration for the inhabitants is to be put first by the Council no extraneous question of sentiment should be allowed to divert the course of justice. It has been derided to hold a special session of the Mandates Commission at Rome, probably in February, to consider the British and French reports on the mandated territories respectively of Iraq and Syria.

Document 9k

[15 December 1925]
The League And Mosul

The text of the report of General Laidoner to the Council of the League of Nations on the incidents on the frontier between Turkey and Iraq is now available. After citing the resolution of the Council in accordance with which he was appointed its representative to inquire into the incidents in the locality of the Brussels line, General Laidoner states that at a meeting of the Sub-Committee of the Council he was informed that his duties would be combined to making an investigation in the district to the south of the Brussels line, as the Turkish Government bad refused to admit a representative of the Council to the area north of the line. He was given entire freedom of action as to the scope of his duties and the means to be employed in conducting the investigation. General Laidoner and the other members of the Commission - namely, Lieutenant-Colonel Jač (Czechoslovakia) and Señor Ortega Núnez (Spain), and two secretaries, left Paris on October 12 for Baghdad, where they arrived on the 26th. Mosul was reached on October 30. There the circumstances of the incidents were investigated in detail and in order to obtain a clear idea of the incidents a visit was made to the frontier zone proper, to Zakho and the places immediately south of the Brussels line. Flights were also made along, the line. General Laidoner sets forth his conclusions as follows:

1. RAID BY TRIBAL AND VILLAGE CHIEFS

Raids made by tribal and village chiefs from one side of the Brussels line into the territory of the State on the other side cannot be regarded as exceptional occurrences. In that very mountainous and wild district almost the entire male population carries arms; the tribes are frequently quarrelling, and some times attack each other in the territory of the same State. Moreover, I found that the provisional frontier, as fixed at Brussels, is not a natural frontier; certain parts of it indeed, are purely fictitious, and can readily be crossed. Accordingly, as the frontier question is at present unsettled, and as it is so easy to cross the provisional line at various points, tribal and village chiefs naturally find circumstances very favourable to brigandage. Although no attack of serious importance has occurred, it is essential to realize that disturbances will always be possible until the frontier question has been finally settled and the line marked out on the ground.

2. OCCUPATION OF CERTAIN VILLAGES BY BRITISH MILITARY POSTS AND PATROLS

From time to time during last summer and autumn the Turkish authorities occupied certain villages to the south of the Brussels line with military posts, and sent patrols there. The British Government, in its protests, mentions the villages of Sinat, Deir-Shish, Nuzur, Sul, Rusi, Hurki, and Mush, and lays special emphasis on the occupation of the village of Nuzur. Accompanied by Lieutenant-Colonel Jač and by two British representatives. Mr. Jardine and Captain Sargon, I visited Nuzur and other frontier villages, and found that the existing maps do not accurately represent the Nuzur area; the villages are not shown in their true positions.

For example, the frontier in the neighbourhood of Nuzur is shown as passing through the confluence of the rivers Geraums and Khabur; the village of Nuzur is farther south (about eight kms.) than the confluence, whereas on the maps it is shown to the north. Very fortunately, however, the Brussels line was described according to the configuration of the ground and the watercourses, and we were thus able to establish the line fairly accurately, and to ascertain on the spot that all the villages mentioned above are situated to the south of it. I think the Turkish local authorities are now pretty well aware of this fact, for there are no longer ally Turkish posts south of the Brussels Line; and if the Turkish authorities refrain from now onwards from sending military posts and patrols into this area, the question of the violation of the frontier might almost be regarded as settled.

3. FLIGHTS OVER THE LINE BY BRITISH AIRCRAFT

As regards the flight over the Brussels line by British aircraft, I am not in a position to express a formal opinion, as I have not been able to make an investigation in the Turkish zone. At the same time, as I mentioned at the beginning of my report, I personally made two flights over the frontier line on November 5 and 17. These two flights were mainly carried out to the south of the Line, and although it is usual in this excessively mountainous district to fly at a height of 9-l0,000 ft. it is fairly easy to appreciate on board an aeroplane whether one is north or south of a certain point, while it is very difficult, if not impossible, to determine the exact-position of aircraft from the ground, on account of the mountainous character of the land and of the height and speed of the machine. Consequently there further remains the possibility that the Turks consider the villages mentioned in Section II. to be north of the Brussels line, but I repeat that in reality these villages are south of the line and have been frequently flown over by British aeroplanes.

4. THE DEPORTATIONS OF CHRISTIANS

With regard to this question I have the honour to report as follows: In the district of Zakho there are at present some 3,000 deported Christians, and every day isolated groups continue to arrive in Iraq. These refugees come from the villages situated in the zone between the Brussels line and the line claimed by the British Government; there are also some who have come from the villages situated north of the latter line. Among the refugees there is even a group of Moslems, but it is a very small one.

I have myself questioned the refugees, but, as I held that this incident in the north of the Brussels line was of considerable gravity, I instructed my assistant, M. Ortega, and the two secretaries, M. Charrère and M. Marcus, to make an exhaustive inquiry among the refugees, to establish the exact circumstances of the deportations. This sub-committee made very detailed and impartial investigations during four days. It interviewed separately people from different villages, of various social class and of different ages and sexes. It also had the advantage of being able to inter- view refugees who came directly from the places from which they were deported, before they had come into contact either with the local Iraq authorities or with their compatriots who were already in Iraq. I regard this fact as very important, because it excludes the possibility of the statements which were made having been influenced in any way. Moreover all the refugee statements are in absolute agreement and may be summarized as follows:

(1) Turkish soldiers, under the command of officers, occupied the villages, and in the first place obtained delivery of all the arms; they then imposed very heavy fines and demanded women - they then pillaged the houses and subjected the inhabitants to atrocious acts of violence, going as far as massacre.

(2) The deportations were deportations en masse, and, according to the statements made, the refugees were conducted to a district farther removed from the provisional line. During the deportations several persons fell ill on the way and were abandoned. Others died of starvation and cold, for, when leaving their homes, they had to abandon everything, and were unable to carry with them either food or clothing. During the inquiry several cases were discovered in which members of families who have taken refuge in Iraq are now in Turkish concentration camps.

This is the general account given by the depositions. We have, moreover, seen ourselves that all those who have arrived are in an absolutely pitiable state. In order to ascertain the real causes of these deportations it would be necessary, in the first place, to hear the explanations of the Turkish authorities; and then to make an inquiry in the localities where the evacuated villages are situated which I have not been able to do. Definite evidence that all the Christian refugees were constrained by force and violence to leave their villages and their homes is, however, to be found in the fact that they have arrived in Iraq without any means of subsistence.

At the present time the situation of these people, in spite of the subsidies of the Iraq Government and the financial help of institutions and private persons in England, is still deplorable. They have lost all their possessions. It is practically impossible to find work for them, and they have nothing to hope for, at any rate for the present. Among all the incidents which have taken place in the zone of the Brussels line, it is beyond question that the deportations of Christians constitute the most important fact, especially if we consider that a fairly large population has been deported from the villages and that these deportations are still going on for as I have already mentioned, further arrivals of refugees in Iraq are taking place every day.

GENERAL CONCLUSIONS

Most of the incidents which took place in the zone of the Brussels line during last summer and autumn are ordinary frontier incidents, inevitable so long as the frontier question is not definitely settled and the line has not been marked out on the spot.

During my stay in Iraq there were no important incidents, and with the exception of the deportations the former incidents were rot repeated. The incidents mentioned in Sections II. and III. of the present report do not, in my opinion, present any importance from the point of view of the decision of the Council. The question of the deportations of Christians is infinitely more important, for these deportations are causing fairly serious and easily comprehensible agitation and nervousness among the Christian population living south of the Brussels line and in the Vilayet of Mosul, and also among the Moslem population of Mosul which favours the claims of Iraq. In conclusion, I feel I must add that the opinions expressed in my telegrams of November 3 and 16 to the Secretary-General and those expressed in the present report are entirely shared by all my assistants.

(Signed) F. LAIDONER. Mosul, November 23, 1925.

DOCUMENT 10
LEAGUE OF NATION REPORT

MISCELLANEOUS No. 15 (1925)
LEAGUE OF NATIONS
REPORT
TO THE
COUNCIL OF THE LEAGUE OF NATIONS

By General F. Laidoner

ON THE
Situation in the Locality of the Provisional Line of the Frontier between Turkey and Irak fixed at Brussels on October 29, 1924

Mosul, November 23, 1925

PRESENTED BY THE SECRETARY OF STATE FOR FOREIGN AFFAIRS TO PARLIAMENT BY COMMAND OF HIS MAJESTY

LONDON: PRINTED & PUBLISHED BY HIS MAJESTY'S STATIONERY OFFICE
1925

CHRISTIAN DEPORTATIONS IN THE NEIGHBOURHOOD OF THE BRUSSELS LINE

Memorandum on the Enquiry conducted between November 8 and 11, 1925, by M. Ed. Ortega-Nunez. M H. Markus and M. E. Charrère.

The refugees who succeeded in escaping deportation by the Turks are distributed in the town of Zakho and the village of Bersivi.

These refugees come from the villages of Billo, Baijo, Alto and Merga, all situated north of the Brussels line.

The refugees from the first three villages were settled, through the Irak authorities, at Zakho; those from Merga at Bersivi. The accommodation is exceedingly primitive, consisting of a simple army tent or mud hut. They are in the utmost physical and moral distress and, owing to the total absence of health persecutions, sickness (malaria and dysentery) is very rife. By the way of help the Iraq authorities allow them each 4 annas a day, which corresponds to about 50 Swiss centimes. In addition, a small quantity of foodstuffs is from time to time distributed to them.

On the 1st of November the total number of refugees was 2,800. It must now exceed 3,000, for scattered groups of fugitives are entering Iraq every day.

The total population of the deported villages was about 8,000 Catholic Chaldeans, whose principal livelihood consisted in agriculture and cattle-breeding. The whole of this population, like all the Christians in Kurdistan, were unconditionally subject to the feudal authority of an "Agha", who was in most cases the owner of the village and absolute master of the life and property of the Christians inhabiting it. Every year the produce of their labour had to be divided in equal parts between the "Agha" extended to the Christians of his village a measure of protection which varied in value according to the number of the inhabitants and the resources of the village.

In spite of these conditions, these people had not complained of their lot.

According to information collected by the Irak authorities, 2,000 inhabitants from these villages have now been deported north of the Brussels line into the Elki district, where they are scattered among several neighbouring villages. In the absence, however, of any information from the Turkish government, we have not been able to ascertain the exact number of those who have died (including those killed) during and since the deportations. From the evidence collected it is to be feared that the number of the latter is very high, and is still growing daily as the result of privation and ill-treatment inflicted upon these unfortunate people.

According to the statement of those who escaped, the deportees who are in the Turkish concentration camps are entirely without resources. Their only food is a handful of barley distributed to them by Turkish officers every fortnight, but as soon as this is distributed the gendarmes come along and take it all away from them. The deportees have therefore to live almost exclusively on acorns, which they find on the outskirts of the villages, or upon the charity of Kurds and a few Christian inhabitants more favourably situated. Further, they have no roof over their heads, and hardly any clothes, and that in a country which is very mountainous and where the snow is already lying deep and the cold is intense. In these circumstances it will easily be understood that many of them have died of hunger and cold, and that with the arrival of winter, which promises to be a very hard one, the number of deaths can only increase.

Method of Deportation

The unanimous evidence which we have collected is to the following effect:

1) Turkish soldiers led by their officers began to enter the villages last March almost immediately after the departure of the Commission of Enquiry from Mosul, and these visits have been since repeated on very frequent occasions.

2) On their first visit the soldiers were satisfied with demanding a sum of money varying in amount in each village. On the following visits, however, they became more exciting, and in addition to money also demanded sheep, flour, butter and women. The latter suffered particularly, and on several occasions when their husbands interposed the latter were massacred in the presence of their wives. The same fate befell the women if they offered any resistance to the brutal instincts of the Turkish soldiers.

At Baijo alone forty men are stated to have been suddenly taken away from their families, shut up in a remote building and assassinated in cold blood by Turkish soldiers, who no doubt were anxious not to be disturbed in their orgies by the husbands and parents of the women they intended to outrage.

3) At the beginning of September the villages were surrounded by the soldiers, and after forming up the whole population, a Turkish officer made the following declaration:

"A war will shortly break out between us and the British. As your villages lie on the provisional line, it is very possible that during hostilities you will be killed either by ourselves or by the English. It is therefore better for you to be removed from this danger zone, and the Turkish Government had decided to undertake this removal."

As soon as this statement had been made, marching columns were formed and set off at once. Nobody was authorised or given any material facilities for carrying away anything with them from the villages, either in the form of food or clothing. The columns were in most cases as follows: First the cattle, then the women and children, while the men brought up the rear of this sad procession. During the journey, which varied from six to ten days, no food was given to these unfortunate persons, several of whom fell out exhausted by fatigue, thirst and hunger, and were immediately dispatched by the Turkish soldiers with their bayonets or the butts of their rifles. At their nightly halts the soldiers selected the women they desired and, if their husbands interfered, the latter were immediately killed.

Most of the refugees who are now in Iraq succeeded in escaping, during the deportation, by bribing sentries with a piece of gold in two which they had been able to keep, despite the searched made.

We have separately interrogated the priest, the mayor (Mukhtar) of each village, whenever people, as well as men of different ages, women and children.

We also had frequent opportunities of interrogating fugitives immediately they arrived to Irak, and even before they came into contact with the British or Irak authorities.

The evidence of these refugees as regards the conduct of the Turkish soldiers agrees to a remarkable extent.

All idea of a voluntary emigration on their part must be excluded. The mere fact that they arrived in Irak and are still arriving daily in the utmost physical distress and completely without resources prove beyond dispute that they were compelled to abandon their villages by force and violence. Moreover, if they had remained in their homes, they could quite easily have provided for their material wants even though they were obliged to give half of all they had to their "Agha". They would therefore never have abandoned their homes of their own accord. Besides that, they are strongly attached to their homes, and the loss of their family life fills them with despair. They are simple people entirely uneducated. The village priest is the only person who can read and write Chaldean at all, and even his general education is extremely limited, a few months of religious teaching from the Chaldean Bishop of Zakho sufficing to obtain for him his ordination as priest and his incumbency. It is typical of the complete ignorance of these people that not one of them knows his age, and when we questioned them on this point they invariably replied: "We don't know, for it has never been written down."

They showed no hesitation in replying to our questions and we never found any contradiction at all between the statements made by persons of the same village. In face of their obvious simplicity, there can be no questions of any previous agreement between them as to the statements they would make.

The Christian populations in question have not as a rule been illtreated by the Kurds. On several occasions the latter even encouraged or protected deportees in their fields to Irak. Furthermore, from information which we have received, but which we could not check because we were unable to carry out any investigations north of the Brussels line, the Kurdish Aghas themselves protested to the Turkish authorities against any deportations, not from any humanitarian feelings, but because of the loss which they sustained through the departure of the Christian population, which constituted their principal labour market. According to information obtained from different sources, the Kurdish chiefs received a communication from the Turkish authorities shortly before the deportations, ordering them to massacre all the Christians in their villages. The Aghas then met to adopt a common policy and to determine what measures they should take. On the proposal of one of them it was decided that this order should not be obeyed, for, to use their own expression, it would have meant the "amputation of their own arms." For this refusal several Kurdish chiefs are said to have been shot by the Turks. Some succeeded in escaping from this fate by fleeing to Irak, but they had to leave their villages and all their possessions. We saw some important Kurdish chiefs of Moslem faith belonging to the tribe Goyana (living on the borders of the frontier), who have taken refuge in Irak and who sought us out on order that we might convey to the League of Nations their wish to have their territory placed within the frontiers of Irak, which they considered, could alone secure for them their life and safety.

I have the honour to give below a short summary of the statements made to us with regard to the actions of the Turks by the refugees of the different villages:

1) Billo, a Village of Seventy Houses
The Turks came for the first time in June, surrounded the village, prevented the inhabitants from leaving it, and imposed a fine of £T. 100 and forty sheep. They then plundered the crops, which they made the villagers themselves to carry to Goyan, two hours distant from Billo. They went off, leaving in the village a picket of about thirty soldiers under Zaky Bey and Saaim Effendi. The chief object of this picket was to watch the inhabitants and observe their comings and goings. The soldiers counted all the persons who went out the village to work in the

country, and if any were found to be missing in the evening, they beat the Mukhtar.

On a second visit the soldiers demanded 100 sheep, which were immediate given them. On the 8th of September, the village was surrounded by about 800 Turkish soldiers. The inhabitants and all the cattle were collected in the centre of the village, while the soldiers plundered the houses. Nine women were outraged; three other had suffered the same fate in August at the hands of the Turkish officers and had been deported.

The day on which Billo was plundered (8th of September) the inhabitants were ordered, through their mayor, Yo, son of Mansur, to leave. The reason given was that as was war going to break out between Turkey and Irak it was better for them if they did not wish to be killed to be deported into the interior of Turkey. Thereupon, the inhabitants were formed up in column with Turkish soldiers on either side. On the evening of the same day the column arrived at Ekrur. The women were separated from their husbands and outraged. Those who attempted to resist were put to death. This scene was renewed on each of the ten days that the journey from Billo to Gueznah lasted. Those who fell out by the way, exhausted by hunger and fatigue, were immediately despatched by the soldiers with blows from their rifles.

The Turks had originally indented to conduct these people to Van, but they were unable to carry out this plan as considerable snowfalls blocked the passages through the mountains; they were therefore obliged to leave the deportees at Gueznah.

On the 1st of November about 220 villagers of Billo succeeded in escaping and in taking refuge at Zakho, and although exact details are not available, it is probable that over 370 inhabitants of the same village are now deportees in Turkey. This number does not include those who were massacred or who died of their privations.

2) Baijo, Village of 200 Houses

The Turks arrived in this village at the beginning of September and installed themselves there. About two weeks later they summoned Paulus the priest, son of Satha, Xymer the Mukhtar, son of Korio, and a number of other village notables and ordered them to hand over all their rifles. The priest was kept as a hostage and was threatened with being burned alive if all the riffles were not handed over within two hours. To show their determination to carry out this threat if need be, the soldiers placed a can of petrol in from of him. Meanwhile, other soldiers established themselves in his house and outraged his wife. Nor did the Mukhtar escaped persecution; he was beaten with cudgels all the time the search for the riffles lasted. The Turks left this village after taking 140 riffles. Five days later about 350 Turkish soldiers under Djemal Bey, Fassin Bey, Nazi Bey and Hamdi Bey surrounded the village. During the night they chose forty of the handsome women. Their husbands were shut up in an isolated place and massacred.

The deportation did not begin until six days after the occupation of the village, but the soldiers had previously massacred the old men, the sick and the children whom they judged incapable of following the convoy. The same fate was meted out those who fell on the way.

Among the evidence taken was that of a certain Ezaie, son of Aurava, and father of three children, one of whom was killed on the way. His wife, who was pregnant and who had fallen ill during the march, was killed before his eyes. His brother-in-law, Isho son of Zaharick, met with the same fate.

One of the families which, suffered most was that of the mayor of the village. Of the 100 members of this family only thirteen were able to reach Zakho; the others were all massacred by the Turks. Moreover, his four sisters were taken by the soldiers, and are at present at Gueznah within the other deportees.

This village was one of the richest in the district and possessed 10,000 head of cattle, all of which have fallen into the hands of the Turks.

On the 1st of November, 348 inhabitants of Baijo had taken refuge at Zakho and the number of deportees in the Elki district is put at over 550.

3) Alto, a village of thirty houses and ten families

An officer and ten Turkish soldiers appeared at the beginning of September and surrounded the village. They gave the inhabitants two hours to hand over the harvest stored in the barns. The ten families were then shut up in a single house, where they remained for three days without any food. Meanwhile, their houses were pillaged by the soldiers. During this process four men were killed, namely Marko, Shamme, Nazi and another whose name we were not given, together with seven women: Zeito, Shimun, Mansur, Tahlia, Amar, Warde and Meero.

The inhabitants of this village were taken towards Begauda. The column was formed up in the following order: the cattle, the men, the children and the women. The latter were subjected on repeated occasions to the outrages of the soldiers.

The deportees heard the Turks say that they were being driven from their village because they were Christians. "We have already done it in other parts of Turkey," they said, "and now it is your turn."

4) Merga, Village of 200 Houses

The Turks came to this village on four different occasions. In March they took straw, 25 mules and 12 donkeys.

In June they took 150 riffles and seized 60 men, whom they bound, telling them they would all be killed if 60 or more riffles were not given up. They also demanded 100 measures (a measure = 13.5 kilog.) of corn and barley.

In July they took 50 measures of barley, 100 sheep and 60 head of cattle, and demanded the payment of 150 Turkish gold pounds. Two men were killed; 4 women were taken by the officers, kept for over a month and rendered pregnant.

At the beginning of September the village was surrounded by 500 soldiers under Colonel Backi and the following officers: Sidquy Bey, Machaat Bey, Salin Effendi, Ismahin Effendi, Majid Effendi, Sukry Bey and Sadrey Effendi. The deportation began immediately. The women were separated from the men and from the children, and the column set out between two files of sentries. Two men, 40 years of age, Ushara, son of Wardie, and Lisham, son of Markhaie were killed in the village when the column was being formed up. Five women, between 40 and 50 years of age, Narian, daughter of Zaya, Warde, daughter of Tando, Yammo, daughter of Marcus, Wuanze, daughter of Simon, and Souze, daughter of Zouco, who fell on the way, were buried under large stones and left there alive. Three girls were killed and several children abandoned on the way dying of hunger, their mothers no longer having the strength to carry them.

According to information received, there were, on the 1st November, 970 refugees from Merga at Bersivi, and 860 inhabitants of the same village have been deported to Turkey and distributed among the villages of Elki, Gueznali, Beit and Chevad. About sixty persons have already died in captivity. To justify this deportation, the Turks declared that there was going to be a war between them and Irak.

The Turkish officers and soldiers who took part in the deportation and committed the acts denounced in the present memorandum all belonged to the 62nd regiment of Turkish infantry.

Mosul, November 23, 1925

BIBLIOGRAPHY

Akgül S., *Musul Sorunu ve Nasturî İsyani*, Berikan, Ankara, 2001.

Al-Jumaily Qassam & Toprak İ., *Irak ve Kemalizm Hareketi (1919-1923)*, Atatürk Araştırma Merkezi, 1999, Ankara.

Anzerlioğlu Y., *Nasturîler*, Tamga Yayıncılık, Ankara, 2000.

Aprim F., *Assyrians: from Bedr Khan to Saddam Hussein*, Xlibris Corporation, n. p., 2006.

Armale I., *Osmanernas och ung-turkarnas folkmord i norra Mesopotamien 1895 / 1914-18*, Beṯ-Froso & Beṯ-Prasa, Nsibin, Sodärtelje, 2005.

'Atatürk: Kürtlere özerklik', *2000'e Doğru*, 6 November 1988.

Avas İ., *Tarihi Hakikatler*, n. p., İstanbul, 2005.

Bilge Y., *Süryanilerin Kökeni ve Türkiyeli Süryaniler*, İstanbul, 1991.

Calilov O. C., *İstoriçeskie Pesni Kurdov, Rossiyskaya Akademiya Nauk İnstitut Vostokovedeniya Sankt-Peterburgskiy Filial*, Sankt Peterburg, 2003.

Çetinkaya G., 'Milli Mücadele'den Cumhuriyet'e Türk-İran İlişkileri 1919- 1925', *Atatürk Araştırma Merkezi Dergisi*, Vol. XVI, No. 48, pp. 769-797.

Dadesho S. O., *The Assyrian National Question at the United Nations*, Modesto, California, 1987.

Donef R., *Assyrians post-Nineveh: conflict, identity, fragmentation and survival: A study of Assyrogenous communities*, Tatavla Publishing, Sydney, 2012.

_____ "The Role of Teşkilat-ı Mahsusa (Special Organization) in the Genocide of 1915" in Tessa Hofmann, Matthias Bjørnlund and Vasileios Meichanetsidis (Eds) *Studies on the State Sponsored Campaign of Extermination of the Christians of Asia Minor (1912-1922) and Its Aftermath: History, Law, Memory*, Aristide D. Caratzas, New York & Athens, 2011, pp. 179-194.

Eşref A. Ş., *Geçmişten Bugüne Savur*, Savur Belediyesi Yayınları, 2003.

Gündoğan C., *1924 Beytüşşebap İsyanı ve Şeyh Sait Ayaklanmasına Etkileri*, Komal, İstanbul, 1994.

Halli R., *Türkiye Cumhuriyetinde Ayaklanmalar (1923-38)*, Ankara, 1972.

Joseph J., *The Modern Assyrians of the Middle East: Encounters with Western Christian Missions, Archaeologists & Colonial Powers*, Brill, Leiden, 2000.

Perinçek M., 'Bu da özgürlük sloganınız mı? *Aydınlık*, 26 October 2012.

Tahir Kodal, *Paylaşılamıyan Toprak*: Türk basınına göre Musul meselesi (1923-26), İstanbul, Yeditepe Yayınevi, 2005.

Karabekir K., *İstiklal Harbimiz*, I, Emre Yayınları, İstanbul, 1995.

Karsh E. and Krash I., *Empires of the Sand: The Struggle for Mastery in the Middle East*, Harvard University Press, Cambridge: MA, 2001.

Koloğlu O., *Mustafa Kemal'in Yanında İki Libyalı Lider*, Ankara, 1981.

Mumcu U., *Kürt-İslâm Ayaklanması: 1919-1925*, 26th Edition, Uğur Mumcu Vakfı, Ankara, 2005.

Nur R., *Lozan Barış Konferansının Perde Arkası (1922-1923)*, Örgün Yayınevi, Istanbul, 2003.

Parhad S., *Beyond the call of Duty*: the Biography of Malik Qambar of Jeelu, Metropolitan Press, U.S.A., 1986.

Sakin S., H. and Kapcı Z., 'İngiltere, Nasturiler ve İç Topral Projesi (1919-1922)', *ATAM*, Vol. 5, No. 5, September 2013.

S.d.B. Mar Šamcun, *Doğu Asur Gelenekleri: Patrik Mar Šamcun'un Katli*, Södertälje, 1993.

Şimşir B., *Lozan telegrafları*, Vol. 1, Türk Tarih Kurumu, Ankara, 1990.

_____, *Lozan telegrafları*, Vol. 2, Türk Tarih Kurumu, Ankara, 1994.

Tahir K., *Paylaşılmayan Toprak*, Yeditepe, 2005, İstanbul.

T.B.M.M., *Gizli Celse Zabıtları*, Vol. IV, Türkiye İş Bankası Kültür Yayınları, İstanbul, 1999.

Tümen Z., 'Özdemir Bey'in Musul Harekâtı ve İngilizlerin Karşı Tedbirleri', *Atatürk Araştırma Merkezi Dergisi*, Vol. XVII, No. 49, March 2001.

Türkiye Cumhuriyetinde Ayaklanmalar, T.C. Genelkurmay Harp Tarihi Başkanlığı Resmi Yayınları, Seri No: 8, Genelkurmay Basımevi, Ankara, 1972.

Şadillili V., *Kürtçülük Hareketleri ve İsyanlar*, Kon Yayınları, Ankara, 1980.

Umar Ö. O., *Türkiye-Suriye İlişkileri (1918-1940)*, Fırat Üniversitesi, Ortadoğu Araştırmaları Merkezi Yayınları, No. 3, Elazığ, 2003.

Ünler A. N., *Türkün Kurtuluş Savaşında Gaziantep Savunması*, Kardeşler Matbaacılık, Ankara, 1969.

Wirsen af E., *Från Balkan Till Berlin*, Albert Bonniers Förlag, Stockholm, 1943.

Yacoub J., *Asur Ulusal Sorunu*, Asurbanipal Yayınları, Jönköping, 1993.

Zülal K., 'Cafer Tayyar Paşa', *Atatürk Araştırma Merkezi Dergisi*, Vol. 15, No. 44, July 1999.

Other sources

Bulletin Périodique de la Press Turque

L'Europe Nouvelle

League of Nations Official Journal

The Times

Time

Riksarkivet [Swedish Archives]

Made in the USA
San Bernardino, CA
03 January 2016